"Amber's power and presence as a
electric—or more necessary. Her deft hand and comp
voice help create the breathing space we need in a world that favors
extremes over nuance and winning over community. Amber has a
hard story to tell, but the journey leads her—and us—to a joyful and
thriving existence every person deserves to experience."

—Flamy Grant, award-winning drag queen singer/songwriter

"In *Out of Focus*, Amber Cantorna-Wylde shares her incredible
story through the epicenter of toxic, anti-LGBTQIA+ evangelicalism to an affirming, holistic spirituality with profound authenticity
and bravery. Her insights are captivating, her wisdom is deep, and
her message is one that will continue to bring healing and hope to
countless queer people who are seeking a life-giving faith. Every
queer Christian and ally should read this book!"

—Brandan Robertson, pastor and author of *Filled to Be Emptied:
The Path to Liberation for Privileged People*

"Amber's story is not uncommon, but it *is* uncommon to find someone who has the courage to be so open and transparent. Amber's
story offers important lessons and insights for everyone, and for
those who have experienced something similar, I believe it will
serve as a source of healing."

—Liz Dyer, founder, Real Mama Bears

"*Out of Focus* is a damn powerful read, no matter how you look at
it. Amber generously shares many heart-wrenching glimpses into
her story—ones that all of us in the LGBTQ+ community of faith
deeply resonate with. Her unabashed honesty is incredibly healing,
as countless queer people will see themselves in her struggle. Her
courage to shed light on ideologies and people who continue to do
harm to the queer faith community is breathless and a call to action.
I'm joining her in that call. Read this book, and you will too."

—Stacey Chomiak, author and illustrator of *Still Stace:
My Gay Christian Coming-of-Age Story*

"When Amber first contemplated sharing her story in 2016, a transgender pastor told her, 'Amber, embedded in your identity is a responsibility to be a voice for change.' I believe this book is a fulfilment of that prophetic pronouncement. Reading her accounts of her first love, coming out to her parents, and her struggle with health issues—no doubt partially caused by the stress of living with rejection—should move one to empathy. But what deeply impresses me about Amber's story is the important role I think it will play in the rising tide of LGBTQ+ awareness for the world, including, hopefully, the church."

—David Hayward, The Naked Pastor,
www.nakedpastor.com

"As someone who was raised in an evangelical culture and then espoused its tenets to my own children and scores of youth group teens, *Out of Focus* hit me with a double punch. Amber's story illustrates the mental toll of living as a standard bearer of impossible expectations while underscoring the generational consequences of a system built on misogyny, bigotry, and damaging messages. *Out of Focus* masterfully connects the dots between the seemingly virtuous lessons preached in American churches and the guilt, shame, and desperation black-and-white thinking breeds in so many congregants. It is required reading for anyone longing for a more inclusive and—dare I say—Christlike Christianity."

—Cynthia Vacca Davis, professor, journalist, and author of
Intersexion: A Story of Faith, Identity, and Authenticity

"Amber Cantorna-Wylde is open and frank about her upbringing in the conservative evangelical church. Her emotional journey from a dutiful daughter to queer liberation is at times heartbreaking, but ultimately, she came to terms with the incredible human being God created her to be. This book is a must-read for anyone who is grappling with or has left a faith tradition based on manipulation and judgment. Amber's narrative is compelling and gives us all hope."

—Nicole Garcia, Faith Work Director,
National LGBTQ Task Force

"Everyone should share in the empowering encouragement that *Out of Focus* offers to its readers. Amber Cantorna-Wylde illuminates a way forward toward renewed self-love and acceptance by boldly and courageously telling her story of love, heartbreak, challenges, and ultimate triumph. Thank you, Amber, for shining hope and exposing those dark places of rejection, pain, and shame that are still being inflicted on so many today through religious stigma, bias, and discrimination. By bringing the trauma that is caused by harmful religious messaging out into the light, many will know that they are not alone! And many lives will be saved!"
—Jane Clementi, cofounder, Tyler Clementi Foundation

"Amber Cantorna-Wylde's writing is raw and engaging, inviting readers into the emotional depths of her experience. This memoir doesn't just tell a story—it illuminates the painful realities faced by LGBTQ+ individuals within the Christian community. It also highlights the strength required to forge a path toward acceptance and love. Amber's story is a beacon of hope for those struggling with similar issues and a compelling call for change within the broader Christian world. As a pastor for over forty years, I highly recommend this book."
—Ray Waters, founding pastor, The Village Church

"Amber Cantorna-Wylde's *Out of Focus* is an important and gripping account of delayed self-discovery and eventual overcoming. As someone who knows firsthand the impossible pressure to hide one's inner life that comes with being raised by parents who work in evangelical ministry, I relate all too well to her protracted and painful process of learning to trust herself and reclaim her own story. That story powerfully exposes the extent to which embracing one's queerness after striving to be the 'perfect' evangelical child takes a toll, and I believe that its telling will help younger people learn to love and accept themselves after facing the unfair and impossible burden of choosing between authenticity and faith-based, hellfire-enforced family demands to conform."
—Chrissy Stroop, coeditor of *Empty the Pews: Stories of Leaving the Church* and senior correspondent, *Religion Dispatches*

OUT OF FOCUS

OUT OF FOCUS

*My Story of Sexuality, Shame,
and Toxic Evangelicalism*

AMBER CANTORNA-WYLDE

WJK WESTMINSTER
JOHN KNOX PRESS
LOUISVILLE • KENTUCKY

Portions of this book were previously published in
*Refocusing My Family: Coming Out, Being Cast Out, and Discovering
the True Love of God* (Minneapolis: Fortress Press, 2017).

First edition
Published by Westminster John Knox Press
Louisville, Kentucky

23 24 25 26 27 28 29 30 31 32—10 9 8 7 6 5 4 3 2 1

Photos are courtesy of Amber Cantorna-Wylde, The Picture People, Ellie Dote, Martha Wirth Photography, and KreativEdge Photography.

Book design by Drew Stevens
Cover design by Mark Abrams
Cover art: From Above, 2021 *(oil on canvas),* Campbell, Lee / Private
Collection / © Lee Campbell. All rights reserved 2023 / Bridgeman Images:

Library of Congress Cataloging-in-Publication Data is on file
at the Library of Congress, Washington, DC.

ISBN-13: 978-0-664-26795-7

Most Westminster John Knox Press books are available at special quantity discounts when purchased in bulk by corporations, organizations, and special-interest groups. For more information, please e-mail SpecialSales@wjkbooks.com.

This book is dedicated to Kelly Loving, Daniel Davis Aston, Derrick Rump, Raymond Green Vance, and Ashley Paugh, who lost their lives in the Club Q shooting on November 19, 2022. It is dedicated to those who knew them and loved them, and to every person who has lost an LGBTQ+ loved one to the hands of homophobia, transphobia, and violence.

Finally, it is dedicated to each and every one of us in the LGBTQ+ community who feel alone in our journey and who fear for our safety every day. May the words in this book bring you comfort, and may they shed light on the harmful ways that bad theology directly links to death. May those in positions of power have the courage to use their privilege to create lasting change. And may each of us in the LGBTQ+ community find the love, safety, and belonging that we each so fully deserve.

You are seen. You are held. You are loved.

CONTENTS

Part 3: The Years Since

FOREWORD
Matthew Paul Turner

One of the things I remember most vividly about the fundamentalist church I belonged to as a child is the way my pastor's voice sounded whenever he spoke the word "homosexual" from the pulpit. Now, all of my former pastor's sermons were loudly presented and included moments when he'd scream the promises of God at us. But any time the Lord "pressed upon his heart" to yell at us about what God's promises were for homosexuals, he'd pronounce the word as if it tasted bad, like he was grossed out and gagging just uttering the word. And he never just simply said the word; he always added four or five modifiers in front of it, a handful of adjectives that forewarned the congregation that he was about to say what he believed was God's least favorite word.

That pastor's proclamations about homosexuality created an environment at my church that wasn't just bigoted toward LGBTQ+ people, but a toxic, violent, and harmful place for people who weren't cisgender heterosexual. That pastor's belief system didn't just affect my understandings about homosexuality while I was at church, but also at home—because my parents held the same ideology. Whenever something about homosexuality was mentioned on the news or was being discussed during a talk show, my father's disgust was visceral.

When I first began to fear that I wasn't straight at age seventeen, the loathing my church and family had long expressed for gay people became internalized as self-loathing. Every nonstraight thought that bounced through my mind tempted my curiosities and, at the same time, caused me to feel an uncanny amount of hatred toward myself. I thought for sure that God couldn't wait to throw my sorry soul into the lake of fire, a scenario that—more often than you might think—I'd imagine and fear and believe wholeheartedly was my future.

That cycle became my journey. I was a church cliché in many ways. Like so many LGBTQ+ people who grew up in some kind of evangelical church, I existed in an unhealthy reality that ebbed and flowed between overwhelming fear and anxiety in the best of times to at least two different occasions in which I spent time ideating self-harm. Most of the time, I walked with shame and secrecy as my companions. For almost thirty years, I lived like that, battling seasons of depression, fighting anxiety and occasional panic attacks, believing that I was destined to live my entire story without ever experiencing what it felt like to be fully known.

I was still closeted when I became familiar with Amber Cantorna-Wylde. Upon hearing her story, I felt two very distinct emotions: on one hand I felt so much joy that somebody had found the freedom to wiggle free; and on the other hand, I battled feeling jealous because somebody had found the freedom to wiggle free. Despite my complicated feelings, I reached out and invited her to be a guest on the podcast that I was doing at the time with a friend. As we were recording that segment, I remember marveling at Amber's bravery and her kind yet stoic presence. Yes, I felt jealous, but I also felt excitement for all the ways I imagined her story would help so many closeted folks like myself.

I was forty-six years old when I came out, several years after that interview. It was by far the scariest thing I'd ever done in my life.

Even though I was a middle-aged man who'd long let go of his once tightly held evangelical belief systems and had, for many years, wholly embraced a progressive theology that was fully LGBTQ+ affirming, accepting my own gay orientation was a layered and complicated struggle for me.

At the time, I was married to my best friend, Jessica. She and I had three incredible children. And while our marriage wasn't perfect, the love and connection that Jessica and I shared with each other was deep, earnest, and real. The thought of wounding Jessica's spirit or causing my children pain overwhelmed me. But the truth is, the longer I avoided my own story and the decades of trauma that my religious ideologies created, the less present I was for the people I loved the most. In my forties, I hit a wall in which I began losing elements of who I was. I became a shell of the human that Jessica fell in love with and married.

It was during therapy that I began to realize that the trauma I carried and allowed to diminish me was slowly becoming a trauma for every member of my family. Eventually, Jessica and I knew what we had to do. But gosh, doing it was so much harder than we'd imagined.

I knew that I was going to lose a lot in the process of telling my truth. And in those moments when I was still imagining all the things that I'd lose, it was impossible for me to consider that I might also gain something in the telling of my truth. But I pushed through every fear, sometimes very clumsily so. And as a friend told me in the days that followed my coming out, "Matthew, you survived the telling. You survived."

One of the first people to text me after I came out was Amber.

But becoming free enough to speak your story out loud is just a beginning. In my first therapy appointment after I came out publicly, after I'd cried about all the things I'd experienced in the last few weeks, my therapist said, "The scariest part is over, Matthew; and now we can begin working on the hardest part—you learning how to love yourself fully and completely."

It's on that journey, the one that put me on a path toward loving myself fully, that I began to get brave.

At some point between coming out and writing *Out of Focus*, Amber Cantorna-Wylde found love for herself, the kind that makes you strong and brave and powerful.

That's what you're about to experience in the pages of this book: a brave and powerful pontification, a story and a telling that are stronger and more potent than the evangelical toxicity and hate-mongering they call out. Amber's truth in *Out of Focus* is light for a church overcome with fear, and life for the souls that fear has tried to diminish.

AUTHOR'S NOTE

The story you're about to read is my own very personal journey of growing up in the heart of the evangelical movement and discovering that who I was meant to be did not fit within the confines of my religion or family system. I have gone to great lengths to be as vulnerable, honest, and transparent as possible. While no one's memory is perfect, I have relied on hundreds of letters, emails, photographs, and journal entries to support the documentation of my story so as to convey it in the most authentic and truthful way possible. At times, events or conversations were combined for narrative flow; quotation marks are used as tools for presenting recollections and should not be regarded as verbatim quotes from individuals. I recognize that their memories of the events described in this book may be different than my own. In addition, the names of many of the people close to me as well as some places have been changed or disguised to protect privacy.

One name has not been changed. That is the name of my father.

In all my years of LGBTQ+ advocacy, I've been careful and intentional about protecting the name, position, and privacy of my father. It felt important at the time for numerous reasons. A lot has changed over the last decade—culture has shifted, data and resources have expanded, we've lived through a Trump presidency and a global pandemic, and the organization of Focus on the Family continues to perpetuate messages about queer people that harm their relationships, their families, their employment status, their mental health, their proximity to faith, and their most basic human rights.

After seven years of working with queer people who have been harmed by religion, it felt critical to my spirit in writing this book to speak loud and clear. To hold accountable institutions that harm innocent people. To call out complacency and complicity. To tell my story. To hope for change.

I know that by naming my father, I open myself up to a host of criticisms, hate mail, misunderstandings, and backlash. I do not name him with malice or because I desire to be cruel or to attempt revenge for my suffering. Rather, I do it to call for justice, equality, safety, and equity for LGBTQ+ people. May my voice and my story be used to reduce shame and isolation for queer people who come behind me, and may they feel a little safer in the world because of it. May this story soften your heart, open your eyes, and call you into deeper justice and love.

Trigger warning: Self-injury is described in detail in several chapters of this book. Each paragraph in which it is discussed is marked with an asterisk (*). Mentions of suicide, although not discussed in detail, are marked with an asterisk as well. Please keep yourself safe and skip these paragraphs if you feel that reading about self-injury or suicide may trigger you.

PROLOGUE

On November 19, 2022—the eve of the Transgender Day of Remembrance—a twenty-two-year-old entered Club Q in Colorado Springs just before midnight, killing five and wounding more than seventeen others before being taken down by patrons. This tragic loss of life and safety has shaken not only the Colorado Springs queer community, of which I am a part, but the LGBTQ+ community at large. Once again, we were the target of a hate crime—desired to be erased from existence.

This is not the first time. The Pulse nightclub shooting in Orlando, Florida, in 2016 took the lives of forty-nine people and injured fifty-three more, making it the deadliest mass shooting in US history at the time. Countless other individuals have lost their lives to violent homophobia and transphobia. Some names we are familiar with, like Matthew Shepard and Tyler Clementi. Many (especially transgender women of color) go unnoticed, unrecognized, and are all too quickly forgotten. The fact that the horrific Club Q assault took place in Colorado Springs feels symbolic of hate coming full circle—from the harmful beliefs and teachings of evangelical ministries headquartered in my hometown to an assault rifle in the hands of a young adult taking innocent lives.

Just five days after the massacre, a message was spray-painted on Focus on the Family's property: *Their blood is on your hands. Five lives taken.* This message, written on a stone wall featuring the organization's name, speaks to the deep level of oppression, disempowerment, anger, fear, and grief that LGBTQ+ people have experienced for years as a by-product of the exclusionary teachings that Focus on the Family has taught and propagated for decades. *It has to stop.* The narrative must be changed. Far too many lives have been taken, both by hate crimes based in toxic rhetoric, and by internalized homophobia and transphobia programmed into queer people from infancy—all in the name of God and love.

The teachings of Focus on the Family value and elevate certain families while simultaneously tearing others apart—teaching tough love, shunning into submission, and reparative therapy in order to fix, change, or heal queer people of their detestable desires. When it doesn't work (because it *doesn't* actually work), parents are instructed to kick queer children out of the family unless they change, in an effort to save their own souls from damnation by association.

I've experienced these teachings firsthand. Raised inside this institution as the daughter of a prominent Focus on the Family employee, I was reared on James Dobson's tough love and molded to put family and God above all else and at any cost. Because of this inside exposure, my childhood was intensively shaped by this organization and its teachings. I was programmed to believe that if I followed a certain formula, my life would be blessed by God and I would be used for greatness. I did all the things. I followed all the rules. I had daily quiet times, I spent hours in prayer, I fasted, I served, and I was active in church. I did discipleship training programs and service trips. I dedicated my life, my time, and my passions to God, suppressing my own feelings and desires in order to serve others. I strictly followed the tenets of purity culture, never dating or even having my first kiss until I was in my twenties. I did everything I was taught to do. But instead of leading to a life of happiness and "blessed-ness," it deteriorated my mental health, chipped away at my confidence and self-worth, and led me into a downward spiral of self-hatred, self-harm, and suicidal ideations. What was supposed to keep me focused on my family ended up tearing me away from them, causing me to be disowned by the people I needed to love me the most.

My story is not uncommon—not yet. I meet people every day in the advocacy work that I do whose stories share similar threads of abandonment, discrimination, and ostracization at the hands of those who claim to love them. It's tragic and it's lethal, taking something as pure and simple as love and turning it into a weapon of division that religion and politics use to pit conservatives against liberals, parents against children, and theology against basic humanity.

In 2016, when I first contemplated sharing my story, a transgender pastor looked me in the eye and said, "Amber, embedded in your identity is a responsibility to be a voice for change." Those words resounded in my soul as if they were directly from the Divine, and they've never left me. I've been striving to be that voice ever since.

We are at a point in history when urgency, accountability, and calling out injustice, oppression, and complicity are critical. It's time to fight for the dignity and life of *every* human being, and not allow our voices to be silenced. I still believe that embedded in my identity is a responsibility to be a voice for change. In this season of urgency, I also believe that *revealing* my identity—my proximity to Focus on the Family and the fact that I was raised on the inside of this system—is how I *continue* to be a voice for change. In doing so, it is my hope that by living into my responsibility, we can someday all live freely, safely, and unashamed.

My father is Dave Arnold, executive producer of *Adventures in Odyssey* and *Radio Theatre* at Focus on the Family, and this is my story.

PART 1

TOXIC EVANGELICALISM

Chapter 1
MY ADVENTURE IN ODYSSEY

"Hi, this is Chris! Welcome to *Adventures in Odyssey*!"

The enthusiastic greeting, followed by the easily recognized *Adventures in Odyssey* theme song, was the backdrop of my life from the time I turned three. I can still hear Chris's cheerful voice in my head, as well as those of other classic characters like Mr. John Avery Whittaker, Connie Kendall, and Eugene Meltsner. I was barely seven the first time I got to play one of the audio characters.

"We're ready for you, Amber. Let's head on back to the studio and get you set up."

Hopping off my stool, I followed the recording engineer back to the booth where a world of "discovery, imagination, and excitement" awaited me.

"Have a seat right here, honey, this microphone's for you," my dad said, placing the headphones over my ears and adjusting the wide black strap on top, my head bobbing a bit at the weight. As an earphone went over each ear, the suction muted all sound, causing the world to go silent. Then, a loud, clear voice from within the earphones broke the dead air. The voice came from a man on the other side of the glass where all the engineers sat in front of the mixing board, ready to record.

"Okay, Amber, let's test the microphone. Do you have your script?"

"Yes, but I already know my lines." I smiled with pride. "All right, then here we go!"

I was a homeschooled second-grader. While most kids listened to the popular kids' audio drama *Adventures in Odyssey* on the radio or (in the early days) on cassette tapes, I was watching it be created in real time. My dad was one of the original *Adventures in Odyssey* staff members, and I loved visiting the recording studio at the Focus on the Family headquarters in Colorado Springs, Colorado, where he worked. The script on the music stand in front of me was another chance to venture into the enchanting world of Whit's End and create something that was listened to by Christian families around the world.

I knew every episode by heart. I could tell you every title, story line, and cassette or CD package it was released on. I used them to help me fall asleep at night, make cleaning my room a little easier, and gauge the remaining time on a road trip.

The excitement of playing one of the characters was matched only by seeing the details of how the episodes were created. I loved watching the actors record and listening as the voice parts were mixed with music to create smooth transitions between scenes. I'd sit behind the mixing board with my dad and watch as actors like Hal Smith, Will Ryan, and Katie Leigh did multiple takes to get the energy just right in a scene. My favorite part of the creation process was Foley (the sound effects). The Foley room was full of props and square cutouts in the flooring, each revealing a different type of carpet, tile, concrete, or walking surface to mimic different environmental sounds. Scattered around the room were a variety of shoes, jackets and coats, ropes, bells, boxes of cornstarch, and pretty much anything you could imagine to create the sound effects that make a story come to life. My dad always came home exhausted after Foley days when he and a coworker acted out each scene and recorded it with a mic to pick up the footsteps, handshakes, sighs, hugs, and doors that opened and closed—all in effort to auditorily transport you to that place in your mind's eye. It was magic, and I loved it.

But the "world of discovery, imagination, and excitement" didn't just live within the fantasy of Whit's End; it also lived within my everyday life at home with my parents and younger brother, Daniel. From the time I was very young, I was taught the utmost importance of one thing: family.

"Cherry Coke, Daddy! Cherry Coke!" my toddler heart begged from inside the nursery of our home in Kalispell, Montana. I pulled at my dad's pant leg and looked up at him until he relented. Smiling down, he picked me up, threw me up in the air, and caught me. I'd giggle and say, "Again, Daddy! Again!"

For as far back as I can remember, I was the apple of my father's eye. From butterfly kisses to Looney Tunes and Saturday-morning cuddles to Cherry Cokes, we shared a special bond that can only be created between a dad and his little girl. He found joy and a connection with me as his only daughter, and with a twinkle in his eye, would often look at me and say, "I'm so proud of you, Am."

My parents worked hard to instill the values that Focus on the Family (FOTF) deemed important. Following the complementarian model of family relationships, my dad went off to work while my mom was the homemaker who raised my brother and me. We were the quintessential family. Homemade meals eaten around the table together, family devotions, a clean and cozy home, and systems for just about everything that kept our lives running in clockwork fashion. That's how you focused on your family.

With James Dobson held up as an expert filled with wisdom that allowed him to speak on God's behalf, Focus on the Family was revered as the prime authority on family, marriage, and social issues. Wondering if that movie is okay for your teenager to watch? Read the review on *Plugged In*. Need something wholesome and clean to entertain your kids? Let them listen to *Adventures in Odyssey*. Having trouble with one of your children acting out? Read Dobson's book *The Strong-Willed Child*. It was the institution that had all the answers to your faith and family needs.

Founded by James Dobson in 1977, FOTF was originally based in southern California. Its mission statement was, "To be led by the Holy Spirit in sharing the Gospel of Jesus Christ with as many people as possible by nurturing and affirming the God-ordained institution of the family and proclaiming biblical truths worldwide."[1] What many people don't know is that prior to founding FOTF, Dobson was a protégé of Paul Popenoe—an atheist eugenicist. Paul Popenoe, who founded the American Institute of Family Relations in 1930, advocated for the forced sterilization of "weaklings" (people with mental illness) in order to improve the race by preventing the "unfit" from being born. In a 1915 article in the *San Francisco Examiner*, Popenoe is quoted saying, "The only hope for permanent race betterment under social control is to substitute a selective birth rate for nature's selective death rate. That means—eugenics."[2] In an effort to make straight, cisgender, healthy White people dominant, Popenoe promoted sterilization procedures that were performed on thousands of people.

But preventing procreation of the "unfit" was only part of the eugenicists' plan. They also had to increase production of the "fit"—White middle-class families. By the middle of the 1930s, the Great Depression was at its height and both marriage and birth rates were in significant decline. So in order to prevent "race suicide," Popenoe shifted his focus from sterilization to marriage and family therapy.

Although Popenoe was not religious, evangelicals became his professional allies in a quest to promote patriarchal and complementarian family values. Popenoe focused on working with religious leaders in "pastoral psychotherapy"— enter James Dobson. Dobson served as Popenoe's assistant at the American Institute of Family Relations. Dobson then launched a film series titled *Focus on the Family*, which Popenoe widely acclaimed. It released in Santa Cruz in 1979, not long after Popenoe's death. While Popenoe is not well-known and may generally be forgotten, his legacy lives on in Dobson and the tenets that FOTF advances.

Popenoe's racist, homophobic, patriarchal idea that healthy White people should be the Super Race not only influenced Adolf Hitler and the Third Reich,[3] but it continues to influence millions of evangelicals today due to the global influence that FOTF maintains. The central idea is that in order avoid "race suicide" and ensure that White Christians stay the dominant race and religion, they should breed as many "culture warriors" as possible. These culture warriors would, in time, grow up and defend the same beliefs as their parents. In *Jesus and John Wayne*, Kristin Du Mez states, "Outbreeding opponents was the first step to outvoting them, and in their reproductive capacities, women served as 'domestic warriors.'"[4]

Encouraging women to stay home and raise children kept straight White men in positions of power and women out of the workforce, ensuring the continuation of patriarchy. It also created a breeding ground that, through homeschooling, molded children from infancy into exactly what evangelicals wanted them to be—sexually pure, patriarchal, homophobic, Christian nationalists, who use their strong beliefs and voting power to fight the culture wars at hand—from integration in the mid-twentieth century, to abortion and LGBTQ+ rights, and most recently, critical race theory in schools.

This piece of history is important to understand because of how it influences my story—and perhaps yours too. In our household, everything came down to one foundational principle: love and serve God above all else. This, by default, included raising a godly family. The ways that eugenics were embedded in these two principles were subtle, but the roots were strong.

My parents made modeling these values their top priority. With the belief that family is more important than work, they strove to be present in the lives of me and my younger brother as we grew up. Thankfully, working at FOTF allowed my father more leeway than many when it came to being an active parent. He'd often be the one to tuck me into bed at night and read or tell me a story. My favorites vacillated between the "Pizza Man" where he'd roll me out like pizza dough and throw me up in the air, and the board book *The Little Mouse, the Red Ripe Strawberry, and the Big Hungry Bear*. My dad could do *all* the voices. Then, always praying with me for sweet dreams and protection, he'd often end by singing:

> You're sugar and spice, you're everything nice
> And you're Daddy's little girl[5]

I never doubted that I was loved.

Leaving our safe home near relatives in Montana and accepting a job at FOTF on the outskirts of Los Angeles to launch the *Adventures in Odyssey* radio drama was a risk for us. It was frightening for my parents to move to a big, metropolitan city and leave the comfort of their small-town rural upbringings. They were young parents making a major move with an almost-three-year-old and a baby on the way. This was *not* their ideal place to raise a family. But they did what they believed God was calling them to do— and thirty-five years later at the time of this book's writing, my father is still employed by FOTF.

My parents were both grateful when FOTF relocated to the beautiful city of Colorado Springs in 1991. Anxious to get away from the inner-city feel and into a smaller town, my parents purchased a home in a quiet neighborhood on the north end of the city, only a short drive from the new FOTF headquarters. Situated across from the Air Force Academy, the FOTF campus was a prime location with a beautiful and open view of Pikes Peak and the Rocky Mountain range. Colorado Springs was the epicenter for many major Christian ministries, so it quickly felt like home, and we put down new roots.

Early on, my mom made homeschooling my brother and me her passion. My parents did not want us to be exposed to all that takes place in a public ("secular") school and could not afford a private Christian school. Home-schooling kept us close to the nest and allowed my parents to tailor our education, making sure the curriculum they chose mirrored their Christian beliefs, especially on topics of creation vs. evolution, history, science, and biblical studies and worldview. Homeschooling was popular among Christians in Colorado Springs (for the reasons named above), so we flourished in that environment. Our mornings always started with individual quiet time with God, followed by getting dressed and being ready for family breakfast and devotions at 7:00 a.m. My mom prepared a detailed schedule to keep us on task each day, which regularly included networking and co-ops with other homeschool families, doing art projects and crafts, and going on field trips.

Our days were highly structured, but after lunch, Danny and I could often be found lying on our beds, listening to an episode of *Adventures in Odyssey*. Like a Christian Disneyland for the ears, the twenty-five-minute radio programs kept us occupied and engaged, while teaching us Christian morals like honesty, integrity, and service to others. Although it was a nice break in our day, my mom knew that allowing time for us to listen wasn't just entertainment; it was another avenue for us to learn the values she and my dad were trying hard to instill in us. They used the episodes as a springboard to teach us overarching principles. The episodes taught everything from manners and respect, to loss and grief, to relationships and dependence on God.

In 2014, my father was involved in creating an entire *Adventures in Odyssey* package (twelve episodes) called *The Ties That Bind* "exploring questions about God's design for marriage and family, loyalty, redemption, commitment, and love."[6] Issued with a discussion guide, it provides questions that correlate with each episode to guide parents on how to talk to their children about "God's design for marriage and family." It released in conjunction with FOTF's *The Family Project*—a twelve-session study for adults designed to explore the biblical foundations of the traditional family. The *Adventures in Odyssey* version for kids targets six- to twelve-year-olds. This package, released well after I became an adult (and about two years after I came out), speaks to the calculated way evangelical messages are intentionally being instilled in the hearts and minds of young children. Molding young minds through entertainment is the ultimate achievement. As the children of one of the original creators of *Adventures in Odyssey*, my brother and I were spotlit to be examples of just how well this teaching method worked. And it *did* work. We absorbed it all.

When *Adventures in Odyssey* celebrated its tenth year in 1997, FOTF hosted a special event at headquarters called "New Year's Eve, Live!" where an episode of the show was recorded in front of an audience. Key actors were flown in from Los Angeles, and my brother and I both played a part. Families from all over were encouraged to attend, which meant lines were long, the house was packed, and people buzzed with excitement.

When everyone was in place and ready to begin, the lights went down and the famous theme song came up playing loud and clear. All of us bantered through our lines together, musicians played to transition us from scene to scene, and a couple of guys did live Foley on the side throughout the show so people could see how the sound effects were created in real time. The crowd was fully engaged.

Following the recording, we all sat behind a long table as families lined up to collect autographs. They bought T-shirts, CD packages, and the newly released book, *The Complete Guide to Adventures in Odyssey*, working their way down the line so that each of the actors could sign their mementos from the day.

"Will you sign this for me?" a cute little girl in pigtails asked me, with her Odyssey T-shirt in one hand and her doll in the other.

"Of course," I said with a smile, asking her doll's name as I personalized her T-shirt for her. I was an early teenager at the time, but remembered my doll-playing days well.

As a little girl, I loved dressing up my dolls and playing house. When I was young, a Cabbage Patch Kid affectionately named Holly Dolly was my favorite. As I got a bit older, I gravitated toward the popular American Girl dolls. I've known many people who already knew they were gay by their elementary years—but not me. When I was that age, I imagined a future family very similar to the one I was being raised in. I dreamed of my someday husband, a cozy house, a family of my own to homeschool and raise on the same FOTF foundation I was reared on, and loads of holiday traditions.

My mom had a gift for making the holidays meaningful, special, and full of symbolism. My parents fed our imagination and cultivated our inner child by letting us believe in the tooth fairy, Santa Claus, and the Easter bunny. I remember one year they even went so far as to use powdered sugar to make bunny tracks on our carpet. We did progressive Easter meals, Fourth of July barbecues, birthday celebrations, and Thanksgiving feasts.

In our younger years we even went trick-or-treating—the most memorable being the year I strung a metal coat hanger through my braids so they stuck out like Pippi Longstocking's. But as we got older, trick-or-treating was outgrown and replaced with what became known as the Great Pumpkin Dinner. A combination of pumpkin-carving with friends, a meal made up of all things pumpkin, and a viewing of *It's the Great Pumpkin, Charlie Brown,* this tradition is one that I've carried into adulthood, often hosting a new group of friends each year to enjoy the fall festivities.

But Christmas was my favorite time of the year. From the time I was a toddler, my dad disguised himself as Santa Claus and came to visit us in his red suit each Christmas Eve. Pushing nostalgia as long as I could, I begged him to continue the tradition long past my believing years. The kid in me loved our traditions, sometimes longer than the rest of my family did. They wanted simplicity; I wanted stability. Perhaps there was a piece of me that felt grounded by the rhythm and routine of traditions. Even when emotions swirled inside of me that I couldn't understand or speak aloud, knowing I could count on a certain calendar of events gave me a level of certainty that I needed—an "okay-ness" that said because these holiday markers happened, things were all right somehow.

As a kid, I was oblivious to these deeper emotional connections, of course. What puzzled me was why Santa always came at the exact time that my dad ran to the store to get 7UP for the Christmas Eve punch. As we grew, we loved sitting on his lap for an annual photo and counted on the matching pajamas he brought in his sack. Oddly, I don't remember all four of us ever having the same pajamas. My mom and I had always had a matching set, and my dad and brother had a matching set. Perhaps all four of us matching strayed too far from gender norms. Regardless of how we matched (or didn't), we went to bed each Christmas Eve snuggled up in new flannel warmth, smiling at the fact that Santa had come for yet another year. Trying hard to create not only a family bond, but also fond family memories that we would look back on for years to come, Mom would often tell me, "Amber, friends will come and go, but your family will *always* be there for you."

I believed what she said. Trusting her, I shaped my view of the world around the concept that Cherry Coke and

Santa Claus moments would always be there, and believed that focusing on my family should take priority above all else. I had no idea that in the future, my family would teach me something very different.

Chapter 2
GROWING UP IN WONDER
BREAD WORLD

"Rise and shine, Amber! Give God the glory, glory!" my mom said with a pep as she came into my room early in the morning and opened the blinds for the sun to shine through. Some mornings I'd even get the full song version. (Yes, you know the one. You're welcome.) Those memories are at once both annoying and endearing. Although my dad is the one who worked at FOTF, my mom is the one who implemented those family values at home during the day. My mom loved being a wife, a mother, and a homemaker—and she was good at it. She focused a lot of time and energy not only on homeschooling us, but also in modeling a godly (traditional) family upbringing.

I remember waking up in the morning and seeing both my parents reading their Bibles and praying. They fasted regularly and taught us to do the same—not necessarily with food, but with things like TV or sweets. Meals together at the table were the rule, pizza and a movie on Friday nights were the exception, and breakfast time included family devotions, prayer, and scripture memorization. When I say scripture memorization, I don't just mean random verses like you'd learn in Awana* (which I also did), I mean entire passages

*Awana is an international evangelical organization focused on child and youth discipleship. It emphasizes Christian principles and rewards scripture memorization and Bible knowledge with merit badges similar to those awarded to Girl Scouts and Boy Scouts for outdoor activities or community service.

and chapters of scripture like Psalm 91, Exodus 20, and Proverbs 3. My mom was big on schedules, routine, and measurable productivity. On top of it all, she kept a clean, hospitable, and welcoming home that always felt peaceful and inviting.

The fact that I've carried on holiday traditions like the Great Pumpkin Dinner for almost thirty years after my mom started it is testament to the fact that she excelled at homemaking. I know that every time I get a compliment about how beautifully my home is decorated or what a lovely table I set for my guests, I owe it to her. There are still times when I wish she could see my home and compliment me on how cozy and inviting it is. While I've let go of some traditions and lived more simply in recent years due to limited energy from living with chronic illness, I have a deep appreciation as an adult for the amount of time my mom invested in creating that warm family environment, and I still model it in my own way as best I can.

When I was seven or eight, my mom also started a club for me and other young girls. She teamed up with her best friend, Shaina, hoping that the club would not only help me make some friends as a homeschooled girl in a new town but also provide an opportunity for me to do the things that young girls love. As a group of about eight girls, we had tea parties and sleepovers; we shared girlie secrets and played with dolls. Comprised mostly of homeschoolers, we got together on a monthly basis. After we read the young adult version of a fun classic like *Little Women,* my mom and Shaina followed up the discussion with specific craft projects that paired with the theme of the story. Of course, the ultimate classic in my household growing up was *Anne of Green Gables*. Anne was the epitome of a hopeless romantic, and her dramatic way of waltzing through life drew each of us in time and time again. Therefore, in honor of Anne, we named our club the Green Gable Girls (GGG).

The GGG club played a significant role in my childhood. Many of my fondest recollections are linked directly to a GGG play we put on, a Christmas tea we had, or a mother-daughter event we orchestrated. My childhood was filled with GGG moments, and that became one of the primary ways that my mother and I bonded.

On my sweet sixteenth birthday, my GGG friends were invited over for high tea. Although often stuck hanging out with all us girls, my brother was a young gentleman and dressed up in a suit to escort each of the ladies in upon arrival. Both he and my dad were great sports and served in the role of our butlers for the evening, waiting on us hand and foot as we enjoyed our tea and scones with clotted cream. Then it was storytelling time—only this story was not a memory of the past, but a foretelling of the future. My dad started the story by summarizing the first sixteen years of my life and then thrust my future into the hands of my all-too-willing friends. I sat, a bit embarrassed, as they each in turn imagined a piece of my future, continuing the story from where the last person left off.

In their collaborative tale of my fate, a few things were clear:

My husband would be dashingly handsome.
I would go on a music tour across Europe.
I would serve in music ministry with my husband for
    a long time.
We would have many babies together.

This was my future through the eyes of my dear friends. Kind, generous, and always good for a laugh, they were definitely, as Anne would say, my "kindred spirits." Whatever brought us together, we always enjoyed each other's company. Mom and Shaina both hoped their hard work would foster bonds of friendship to last a lifetime.

Ironically, although I'm sure the circumstances look very different from what my mom envisioned, I *am* still in touch with several of those girls today. In fact, two of them have come back into my life as some of my best friends and strongest allies. Having friends who have known you from childhood and with whom you have shared lived experience is so rare and helpful—especially as we all try to process and heal from the religious trauma we've each experienced. It's a bit of a paradox, but my mom did succeed at creating lasting friendships, even though life placed us back together in a much different place than any of us would have imagined.

Both Mom and Shaina worked endlessly to make our times together not only fun but meaningful and steeped in tradition and symbolism. They also made sure God was at the center of it all by teaching us how to be young women of God and how to develop the traits that Proverbs 31 (in the NKJV translation) says make a "virtuous wife." In fact, my entire high school curriculum was called *Far above Rubies,* alluding to the same verse in Proverbs. There was a separate curriculum for boys titled *Blessed Is the Man,* but for whatever reason, that wasn't used for my brother.

Gender roles were clear. Women were to be homemakers, men were to be breadwinners. My brother was taught how to be a gentleman by doing things like opening doors for girls, pulling out a lady's chair before she sits down, and treating women with gentleness and respect. I was taught how to be a young woman by wearing dresses (complete with pantyhose and a slip beneath the skirt), acting like a lady in both words and mannerisms, and baking desserts. Whether it was in school, at home, or in places like the GGG club, qualities like maintaining a clean house, cooking meals from scratch, being hospitable, being graceful, being patient, sacrificing herself for others, and (brace for it) submitting to her husband were characteristics that were expected of a godly wife and mother. And being a godly wife and mother was exactly what I was being trained to become, even from my youth. Like Wonder Bread, we were White, straight, clean-cut, plain, and always predictable. Etiquette and ladylike manners were important (I remember being scolded for *not* being ladylike the first time I used the word "crap"), but even those traits were secondary to things like self-sacrifice, service, personal quiet time with God, and homemaking skills.

Entering my midteens, these homemaking skills I was being taught (which were fun in my youth because I got to dress up and learn things like bread-baking or cross-stitching from adults I admired) began to morph into ways I had to perform and standards I had to live up to. Since my mom was the leader of the GGG club, a certain expectation developed when it came to my own behavior. These girls looked up to my mother and therefore looked up to me. Often their confidante, I was the one they would go to for support and advice. I even remember one of the girls once saying to me, "With your dad being the producer of *Adventures in Odyssey* and your mom leading the GGG group, your family must just be so perfect!"

No, my family was not perfect. Appearances can be deceiving.

In reality, the pressure I was feeling, from a dad with a well-known position at FOTF and a mom who led the group that all my friends were a part of, was beginning to weigh on me. My mom expected me to lead these girls by example. It was understood that I would always have a good attitude and show up with a smile. Being a *blessing* to these girls was an assumed responsibility. I was supposed to be a positive role model for them. Being pressured into a role of peer leadership made it hard to be just one of the girls.

But "being a blessing" was a standard expectation for every area of life in our household. Whether performing somewhere, going to visit relatives, or hosting company in our home, it was essential to put other people's needs above our own. Before we'd arrive somewhere, my mom always made a point to tell us, "You need to go with the mind-set that you're going to be a blessing to them." What that really meant was to help out and be on our best behavior—the term *blessing* just gave it the Christian trademark.

Blessing others was especially important when it came to our musical gifts. Like Christianity, music was a part of my life from the time I was born. My mom came from a musical family that traveled and sang as a group in her teen years, so she instilled that same passion in both me and my brother from birth. Singing my first solo in church just before I turned two sparked the beginning of a lifetime of musical performances. From that moment on, there was rarely a time when I wasn't involved in a children's choir or performing in some capacity.

After hosting my first solo piano recital at the age of seven and seeing my talent quickly take off, my parents took me to audition for a woman who had obtained her degree from the London Conservatory of Music. A sage woman, she prided herself on being strict but fair, and I met my match in her as she constantly gave me the challenge I sought. Competing in district and regional competitions frequently, I often came home with a blue ribbon or trophy to go with my big smile and sense of accomplishment. In hindsight, I sometimes wonder what my parents saw as my musical end goal. I had a lot of determination and talent for my age, but when I got older and considered music school, they saw it as a lofty dream without a promising career. "What's the point of going into debt over college if you're just going to get married and have babies?" my mother said. Perhaps they saw it as a component of future opportunities or a companion to ministry. Regardless, the financial sacrifices my parents made to foster my musical gifts are still among the things I am most grateful for.

Performing brought me joy. I loved it, and I'm grateful that my mom instilled that passion in me from such a young age. My early childhood experience with music later opened up opportunities for me to travel with both national and international musical groups in my teen years. Music shaped me. It made me come alive, and I always looked forward to the next musical challenge or opportunity. While the Green Gable Girls was where I went to have fun and be girlie, music is where I went to be inspired and challenged. I found comfort in the way the lyrics and piano keys connected me to a form of expression. Since emotions became hard for me to express honestly in my home environment, pouring that emotion into my music lent me strength. I didn't have to find words to describe how I was feeling. Instead, I could show it in the sound my fingers created.

As a teenager, I met a pianist named Lena who transformed the way I experienced music, furthering my ability to explore it as an outlet of self-expression. The way Lena sang and played the piano was so raw and authentic. It wasn't at all like the classical music I played to reflect my buttoned-up life. There was something different about it that I couldn't quite put my finger on. With my training rooted in classical piano performance, I was never exposed to the world of chord charts and improvisation, but the way Lena's fingers danced freely across the keys intrigued me. She decided where they went and how they moved. They weren't dictated by black dots on a staff of lines and spaces. This world was composed of endless possibilities. I was captivated, and I looked forward to hearing her play every week at church. Soon, I was willing to do anything to play like her. I desperately wanted to unlock the same ability inside of me. I felt jealous, and at times even angry, that Lena could play with such freedom when I felt so bound to follow notes on a page.

In hindsight, I see this as a perfect example of how I was feeling about everything in my life at that time. I felt confined, boxed in, restricted, and bound to rules that told me how to live. What I wanted (even though my sexuality was still hiding beneath the surface) was to break loose and be free to live authentically without the need for façades.

When I discovered that Lena taught piano lessons, I persuaded my parents to let me switch instructors. They agreed, provided I continued at least some degree of classical work.

What followed was a realization that, as much as I enjoyed listening to Lena play this new style of music, learning to play it myself was quite challenging. Following rules was embedded in me—not just in my music, but in my life—and figuring out how to create a new pattern of playing, when the whole point was that there was no instruction manual, frustrated me. A small-faceted example of the diversity that was to come later in my life, playing in an improvisational style overwhelmed me, and the perfectionist inside me was impatient at my own progress.

The mold I'd been raised to fit within—it turned out—was very hard to break.

Between Green Gable Girls events and family musical performances, my life was performance-based from the start. Mom devoted a lot of time to teaching Danny and me to sing in three-part harmonies, and by the time I was nine, between our musical repertoire and our scripture and poem recitations, we were putting on entire concerts by ourselves at retirement homes, Christian schools, and local churches. Dad played the role of our supportive sound engineer, and Mom was the model of creativity and service to others.

Regardless of what my mom put her hands to do, blessing others and self-sacrifice were always front and center to her and therefore were taught to be front and center for me. I quickly picked up on the idea that my own wants and needs should always take a backseat to other people's. It created a slow death of my own longing that took place over a period of years. It happened in a way that was subtle and subconscious, covered up with smiles and making others feel good. I didn't even know it was happening until I realized as an adult how hard it was to ask for what I needed emotionally or to take up emotional space in a relationship. "Don't want. Don't need," the voice in my head says to me. "Make yourself small. Don't be too much. Don't ask for *that*. Don't complicate things. Don't create conflict. Don't be a *burden*." These hardwired ideas about how to move through the world have proven difficult to deprogram.

I've also come to recognize that blessing others often came with a hidden caveat. There was an unspoken mentality among evangelicals in general that divided the world into two groups. There was *us* (those who were Christian, those who were homeschooled, those who followed the teachings of FOTF and of God—in other words, those who were *right*) and then there was *them* (the rest of the world— meaning anyone who was not our brand of Christian and therefore not like us). Catholics weren't really Christians. Mormons and Jehovah's Witnesses definitely weren't Christians. Atheists and agnostics needed saving the most. Secular teenagers were rebellious. Those who went to public school were exposed to too much. LGBTQ+ people were responsible for corrupting our society and destroying the traditional (God-ordained) institution of the family. And those who didn't believe in and trust God for their future had a hard road ahead, eventually destining themselves to eternal damnation.

"You should be grateful that you have the family you have, Amber. Most kids aren't as fortunate as you," my mom regularly told me. And in some ways, she was right. There were ways in which I was fortunate. I would later realize there were also ways in which I was very unfortunate. But the problem with this mentality is that it created a hierarchy. Rather than seeing everyone as equal, it ranked us above everybody else. It made us better than them, more knowledgeable than them, more spiritual than them, more *saved* than them.

In turn, "being a blessing" to others became a form of charity—something we did to help those less fortunate than us. And in helping them, the goal was always to bring them a step closer to becoming us. Our gifts of blessing rarely came without strings attached. The unspoken expectation was that whatever we were doing to help them would hopefully bring them one step closer to believing in God our way—the committed, Christ-centered way led by biblical truths according to God's commands . . . as we interpreted it. How sad and boring to think all the world needs to be exactly the same.

Growing up in a silo of White, straight, cisgender, able-bodied, privileged, evangelical Christians who all thought and believed exactly alike did me a great disservice. Not only did I miss out on the opportunity to experience and see the world (and faith) from varying points of view, but I was also denied the opportunity to explore and understand who I was in the world at a younger age.

Now, being a divorced, gay female with an invisible disability, being immersed in a variety of cultures, perspectives, experiences, and faiths, is critically important to me. Some of my best friends are queer, transgender, nonbinary, polyamorous, people of color, people of different faith or no faith at all, neurodivergent, chronically ill, disabled. I love hanging out with the marginalized, not only because I am marginalized myself, but because that is where authenticity, intersectionality, and richness lie. But it was a long time before I felt free enough to explore that.

Closeting emotions as a child was what equipped me to closet my sexuality as I got older. If I expressed disappointment over an event getting canceled, my mom would tell me, "It's better to not get your hopes up in the first place." If I was struggling with something, I was told to pray harder and have more faith. If I was sad, I was encouraged to believe that God would work everything out for my good. I was never allowed to simply *be* and *feel* my feelings. I was always expected to find the appropriate Band-Aid and immediately apply it. It was clear that certain feelings and experiences were better kept hidden and undiscussed. That lesson was reinforced in a devastating way when I was around the age of nine.

In the family room one afternoon, I sat on the couch mindlessly watching a TV show. Our options for unsupervised viewing were mostly limited to *Looney Tunes, The Brady Bunch, Scooby-Doo,* and *Little House on the Prairie,* so whatever was playing on TV had to be G-rated. Yet something I saw that day suddenly triggered a flashback to memories I had managed to suppress for several years. Fear overtook me and panic riddled my small body as I sat on the couch not knowing what to do. Scared and upset, I crawled behind the recliner in the corner, curled up in a ball, and began to cry. A few moments passed before my mom, hearing my tears from the kitchen, came to see what was wrong. Finding me in the corner where I was hiding, she brought me out and sat next to me on the couch.

After composing myself a bit, I took a huge emotional risk and opened up to share a very vulnerable moment with my mom.

"Remember when we lived back in California?" I started, trying to communicate through my tears. She nodded.

"Well, sometimes when I played with Steven next door, we would hide in the back of his mom's big van and . . . ," my voice trailed off.

She waited patiently, not wanting to put words in my mouth but fearing what might come next. After several attempts, I managed to tell her what had taken place on those days we hid in the back of the van: sexual acts that did not make sense to me when they happened at the age of five, nor now at the age of nine as I described them to my mother. Years passed before I was able to piece together that the sexual abuse my neighborhood friend suffered at the hands of his babysitter was being passed on to me (what is now known as child-on-child sexual abuse) in those acts. But as a preteen girl, I described to my mom what happened to the best of my ability, given my extremely limited knowledge and sheltered upbringing, and waited for her response.

She asked a few questions and then, feeling like she had all the necessary information, calmly replied, "Well, honey, sometimes these things just happen. It's natural for kids your age to be curious and experiment."

Curious? Experiment? I may have only been nine, but I knew enough to know that what happened did *not* resonate in my body as an experiment in curiosity. I stared at her in disbelief. Shaken and upset, I was deeply hurt by my mom's response. I felt like she blew off the severity of what I had just shared with her, brushing it under the rug with the other things she didn't want to acknowledge or let anyone see.

This was a crucial turning point in my childhood development. I didn't realize it at the time, but her comments that day undermined the significance of what had happened and severed a tie of trust between us. Not validating me downplayed my pain and taught me that it wasn't safe to share the deepest parts of my heart with my own mother. In that moment, I realized that how I felt and what I was going through took a backseat to comfort and appearances. This was the first in a series of experiences where my mom allowed her discomfort over something I had gone through to minimize the pain I was experiencing. From that moment on, I began compartmentalizing my emotions and hiding how I really felt.

I started realizing that emotions like humility, happiness, and excitement were encouraged to be front and center, while emotions like sadness, disappointment, anger, and fear were meant to be hidden away and never seen. I took notes and began cataloging my feelings accordingly. If I wanted to be loved and accepted by my parents, I had to follow the rules and act as they expected. If I didn't, I subjected myself to their disapproval, punishment, and, worst of all, disappointment in me.

Over time, I withdrew even more within myself. I hid my heart and buried my feelings so that no one could see how I really felt or who I really was inside.

Chapter 3

THE HARMS OF
PURITY CULTURE

I grew up entrenched in the heart of purity culture—an evangelical megamovement and subculture centered on abstinence-only education and the doctrine that sex is holy only in the confines of a straight marriage between a cisgender female and a cisgender male. This movement was marked by True Love Waits campaigns and books like Joshua Harris's *I Kissed Dating Goodbye* and *Boy Meets Girl,* infiltrating the hearts and minds of a generation of youth through conferences, Christian bookstores, purity balls, and teen magazines. This new benchmark for Christian holiness reached its height in the 1990s, which is exactly when I hit puberty.

The messages about sex I remember hearing when I was a teenager consisted primarily of three rules: do not engage in sex before marriage, do not masturbate, and do not put yourself in a compromising position where you may be tempted to go "too far" with the opposite sex. The exact definition of "too far" was a little vague, however, and often fluctuated depending on who you asked. Some people (mostly teenagers) thought everything except penetration was acceptable, while others (mostly parents and youth pastors) said that even simple gestures like holding hands or kissing were going "too far" before marriage.

This notion of saving even the smallest forms of physical connection for marriage was derived from the concept of courtship—a way of getting to know someone of the opposite sex that includes parental involvement and is only done with the intentions of pursuing a person for the purpose of marriage. Although Harris didn't invent courtship, he certainly repopularized it and promoted it as an alternative to dating in his book *I Kissed Dating Goodbye*. Published in 1997—the year that I turned thirteen—it sold more than 1.2 million copies and largely influenced a generation as one of the leading resources in the purity movement. Advocating that it is best to not even kiss until you're standing at the altar, Harris warned about the dangers of "emotional hookups" and proposed a way to "remap [our] romantic lives in the light of God's Word."[1]

Writing at only twenty-one years of age, Harris was a homeschooled virgin, speaking to teens worldwide about "how they can live a lifestyle of sincere love, true purity, and purposeful singleness."[2] Advocating for courtship is deeply problematic in ways that are impossible for a naive twenty-one-year-old kid to understand. One of the gravest issues is that by advocating for youth to refrain from kissing or, in some cases, even holding hands until their wedding day, you rob them of the experience of getting to know themselves and their bodies. If they never experiment or date, how are they to ever know what they like and don't like, what they need or want in a life partner, or what feels good to them sexually? It denies them opportunities to mature and learn valuable lessons in regard to attraction, chemistry, boundaries, and agency.

Rather than advocating for autonomy and agency, this extreme abstinence-only approach teaches youth to fear sex and hate their bodies, rather than explore the good and holy gifts God gave them. For me, I was cheated out of the chance to realize I was gay earlier in life and eventually entered a marriage that, over time, stripped me of both autonomy and agency.

Women are disproportionately affected by this belief system, having our virginity likened to a prize we present to our spouse on our wedding night. If that is lost (due to premarital sex) or stolen (through rape or abuse), or even worse, if we're gay or become pregnant, then we were taught that our sexuality was tainted and stained, rendering us both undesirable and unlovable. Believing this convinced many young people raised in the evangelical subculture, myself included, that once that happened, nobody would ever want us again, causing us to internalize feelings of shame, self-hatred, and worthlessness.

This explains why the child-on-child sexual abuse I experienced as a young girl affected me so deeply. Even before I knew the details of purity culture or understood much about sex, there was one thing I did know: what happened to me as a kid was dirty enough to make my mom want to hide it. For years after that confession, I punished myself with cold showers as penance to make myself clean before God any time I felt guilty over what happened in that van. Repenting for my mistake over and over until I *felt* forgiven, I tried to earn my way back into God's good graces. I suppose you could say I was groomed for purity culture, taking note of every standard this new bible for Christian romance offered so as to align myself as perfectly as possible. My purity may have been tarnished by what happened to me as a little girl, but technically, my virginity was still intact, and I was going to do everything in my power to keep it that way.

At youth group, my pastor compared virginity to a stick of gum. He likened having sex before marriage to

ABC (already been chewed) gum, saying that each person you sleep with is the equivalent of passing on that stick of used gum and picking up all the germs (or sexually transmitted infections) that come along with it. Each time you sleep with someone, you're also sleeping with every person they've ever been with and, at the same time, creating an eternal tie with them. Another popular analogy was likening a girl's virginity to a rose—it starts off beautiful and pure, but if given to someone outside of marriage, becomes wilted, losing all its petals and making you nothing more than a naked stem. These scare tactics were as traumatizing as they were effective.

As a way to further control women and scare them into submission, they layered on the responsibility of dressing modestly, claiming that it was our job to keep the boys from lusting. I can't tell you how many times I heard that "guys only want one thing," which intentionally instilled fear into us as teen girls so we'd remain virgins until our wedding day. It didn't matter where I turned—whether that was FOTF's teen girl magazine, *Brio and Beyond,* or church youth group, or female mentors like those who led the GGG club—the message was the same: sex before marriage is dirty and sinful, and sex after marriage is blissfully perfect and pure, like a switch that flipped from bad to good on your wedding night. The problem, of course, is that the mental switch doesn't actually flip instantaneously. When you've been inundated all your life with messages that tell you sex and your body are bad, getting married doesn't automatically change that internal narrative, no matter how much you want it to. Given no tools regarding how to actually enjoy sex and explore our bodies, many of us were left confused, frustrated, and full of shame.

Although the idea of sexual purity was a message I'd heard all my life, my thirteenth birthday was when it really began to take hold. Thirteen was somehow the magical age that set you apart. It was seen as the beginning of one's journey from girlhood into becoming a young woman. To celebrate this milestone, grandparents, aunts, and cousins came from out of state to be part of my special day, and all my family and friends gathered for this coming-of-age ceremony. It was like an evangelical's version of a quinceañera, steeped in Christian symbolism and expectations for my future.

My father presented me with a purity ring, and I took a vow of purity (sexual abstinence until hetero marriage). This was an expectation as much as it was a celebration. Taking this vow of purity in the presence of loved ones was meant to be memorable and representative of them "bearing witness" to this important commitment. Each person in the room took a turn sitting beside me and publicly sharing a special memory, some age-old wisdom or advice, or a Bible verse. While some of them were undoubtedly a bit awkward, many of them were quite meaningful. I've always loved feeling emotionally connected to other human beings, so this complemented my love language.

The entire day, and even the gifts, were steeped in symbolism. My parents presented me with a hope chest that was meant to store "all my hopes and dreams for the future." This gift, though well-intentioned, undoubtedly pointed to my wedding day and future family, serving as a tribute to a woman's intended place in life. Already stocked with cookbooks and crocheted doilies, it was a place for me to continue collecting and storing my dreams for when I got married and had kids of my own. In the coming years,

I filled the cedar chest with things I hoped to use with my someday family, as well as keepsakes I wanted to pass down to my future children.

Truth be told, I still have that chest, but its use has changed dramatically over the years. For a while, I actually stored memorabilia from my (spoiler alert: gay) wedding inside, giving the whole thing a bit of an ironic twist. But now, it's simply a piece of furniture, the embroidery on the top covered with new fabric to give it a fresh feel, and used to store winter gear in the entryway, where people can sit and put their shoes on to come and go.

For many years, at the bottom of the chest, you could still find the purity pledge I took that day I turned thirteen. In February 2022, I finally tore it up during a live podcast interview on purity culture.[3] I'm not sure why I kept it all those years. Perhaps because I was still looking for a way to transform it into something redemptive.

Before signing the vow that day, my parents spoke about the importance of purity and living a life "holy unto God," and my dad read aloud the pledge that I was about to publicly sign.

> Believing and waiting for God's best, I pledge myself to be sexually pure until I enter into a marriage relationship, ordained by God, and with the person God has chosen for me. Lord, help me to keep this commandment, so that I may honor You, my family, and my future mate.
>
> "Flee also youthful lusts; but follow righteousness, faith, charity, peace, with them that call on the Lord out of a pure heart."
>
> 2 Timothy 2:22

I find it interesting that nowhere did it say "husband" or "man of God." It simply states "a marriage relationship, ordained by God, and with the person God has chosen for me." Somehow its requirement that the person be of the opposite sex was just implied. Obviously, these commercially available certificates found at Christian bookstores were intended to be gender neutral and applicable to "both sexes,"* but looking back on it now as a gay woman of faith, I believe that as queer people, our marriages *are* ordained by God and equally holy to that of marriage between straight people.

Unfortunately, it was many years before I came to terms not only with my sexuality, but with how my sexuality is embedded in my faith. With my entire thirteen-year-old heart, I took the pen in my hand and signed on the dotted line of that purity pledge, intending with everything in me to stay sexually pure until my wedding night.

My dad then opened the velvet box that contained my purity ring. It was sterling silver with a cross, a heart, and a key signifying that Christ held the key to my heart until the day came for me to be married. A father-daughter necklace was also given to me that day, with my chain containing a heart locket, and my dad's chain holding the key. I realize now that this concept is the epitome of patriarchy, which has, for millennia, considered a daughter the property of her father until that ownership is transferred to her husband. This is still symbolized today by the father walking the daughter down the aisle and "giving her away." Not only does it enforce a hierarchical father-daughter

---

*I say "both sexes" here because evangelical culture only honors male and female genders. It does not support nonbinary or genderqueer individuals and therefore is only gender neutral to the extent of including binary male and female genders.

relationship, but it also encourages a hierarchy in the marriage. While it was commonly taught that the rank of priorities should always be God, spouse, children, others (notice that one's self is absent from that list), it was also taught that the husband was the head of the household and that the wife's job was to submit to him as she would to God. Men made the decisions based on God's leadership; women followed without question. This misogynistic way of thinking perpetuated beliefs around women's roles and abilities that are now seen by many as archaic. It also downplays a women's agency, especially as it relates to sex.

I was oblivious to all that back then, of course. Pulling the ring out of its case, my dad looked at me through misty eyes.

"Today marks the start of a new journey for you, Amber—the journey of becoming a young woman. As your dad, I want nothing but the very best for you and I'm so proud of the way you've always put God first in your life. In the years to come, your mom and I promise to stand by you and coach you along as you navigate the many challenges that lie ahead. As you wear this ring, let it be a compass that guides you throughout your life; a constant reminder of the pledge you've made before God, your family, and your friends. I love you, and I'm so proud to be your dad."

He placed the ring on my ring finger (yes, my left hand, where my wedding ring would one day go!) and wrapped his arms around me in a long embrace. Everyone gathered around, laid hands on me, and prayed over me to seal the commitment I had just made. As they did, I felt the weight of responsibility heavy on my shoulders.

Throughout my teen years, I wore that ring with pride and every intention of keeping my vow. I took my commitment seriously and planned on fulfilling it. I'd often tell myself that I wasn't dating because I didn't want to put myself in a compromising situation. But the truth was, I didn't have any desire to date. Even during puberty, I had no interest in boys. Perhaps that should have been a sign to me of things to come, but it wasn't. I was naive, and my lack of education, experience, and exposure kept me unaware of the reality of my own desires.

I watched many of my friends go through the cycle of dating, breaking up, and having their hearts broken, only to repeat the process over again ad nauseam. I was thankful that it wasn't me. I convinced myself that I was grateful God had saved me from all that heartache, even when I found myself lonely. I knew in due time, if I was patient, remained true to my vow of purity, and faithfully served God with my life, God would reward me with my knight in shining armor. In some ways we treated God like a slot machine—promise in, reward out.

Purity was an assurance that happiness was in my future.

Staying pure was what every good Christian teenager was supposed to do. So, with a desire to please God, my parents, and those I respected and admired most, I followed suit. The purity vow cemented in me early on that, according to my FOTF upbringing, there was only one acceptable way to love and only one version of a godly Christian family. Having no exposure outside this evangelical cocoon and no other frame of reference for sex or sexuality, I bought into this lie hook, line, and sinker.

Today, I see purity culture for the gaslighting ploy that it is. That may sound harsh, but when something has been so emotionally traumatizing and psychologically damaging to so many, it's important for the dignity of those affected to call it what it is. Millions of Gen Xers, millennials, and Gen Zers, regardless of sexual orientation or gender identity, are working hard to undo the harmful messages they internalized as a result of the information they received in their youth. The damage is extensive. More of a scare tactic for chastity than a doctrine of theology, it carries deeper messaging than just the value of abstinence for the sake of health and delayed pregnancy. It reduces one's identity to their sexual purity and virginity, making one believe that they are worthless without it, rather than seeing it as simply one part of their entire being.

For many, that has caused great harm in their romantic relationships as they entered adulthood, causing them to rush to the altar too early or too young, just so they can say they were a virgin on their wedding night. On the flip side, it has caused great guilt and shame long into what should have been healthy marriages, simply because one or both partners couldn't flip that mental switch to suddenly make sex pleasurable and good upon completion of their wedding vows. This confusion and shame also create distance in one's relationship with God in the process as they continue to wrestle with stigma about sex and their bodies—a body actually designed by God and intended for pleasure!

In 2018, Harris removed *I Kissed Dating Goodbye* from publication, and in 2019, he divorced his wife and denounced Christianity, embarking on an apology tour to try and reduce the damage. While this may be helpful for slowing down purity trends in the current and forthcoming generations, millions of people are still grappling with the damage already done and are unsure how to rewire their thinking when it comes to dating, sexuality, their bodies, and healthy sex. It angers me that Christian ministries like FOTF and True Love Waits used a kid, with no life experience in either dating or marriage, to promote their abstinence-only agenda. The damage done far and wide is irreparable.

It's imperative that we develop a new system of sex education in faith spaces, like the Our Whole Lives (OWL) program developed by the United Church of Christ, which encourages healthy exploration of one's own body and teaches that there are many ways to create a loving family. Being taught that there was only one kind of family stunted my growth so that I was not able to recognize and appreciate the diversity in all families, or to recognize and appreciate the diversity within me.

I wish I could say that, deep down, I had an inkling about my sexual orientation back then (because it sure is obvious to me in hindsight), but I didn't. Words like *gay* and *straight* weren't even a part of my vocabulary or concepts that I understood. I had no idea what it meant to be gay other than that "those people" were supposedly against everything that we stood for—mainly God and family. They were seen as liberal partiers, drunkards, sexually loose, opposed to God and religion, and fussy about politics and equal rights. Somehow my parents managed to paint this ugly picture of LGBTQ+ people in my head without ever exposing me to them—which is exactly why it worked, keeping me oblivious and closeted for over another decade.

Chapter 4
EXPANDING HORIZONS

Turning thirteen was a monumental time in my life. Not only did I take a vow of purity and make a commitment to abstain from sex until marriage, but I also discovered a new church and with it, a redefined understanding of God. It was a transitional period for me as I entered young adulthood, but it was also a transformative time for my faith.

As a child, my beliefs were shaped by the beliefs of my parents. As a teen, I began developing a faith centered on my own relationship with and understanding of God. Granted, that faith was still strongly molded and influenced by those in evangelical leadership—at youth group, at church, through worship music and contemporary Christian music artists, and from mentors whom I looked up to, admired, and emulated. Living in a Christian cocoon could produce nothing else. There was no exploration outside of evangelical beliefs, but my faith became more three-dimensional, as opposed to flat text on the pages of an NKJV or NIV Bible. Centered Life Church opened my eyes to a whole different dimension of evangelical Christianity and quickly became the place where I spent most of my free time for the next thirteen years.

The first time I ever attended a service at Centered Life was with Shaina, the coleader of the GGG group. After pulling into an empty parking space in the spacious lot on the north end of the campus, Shaina held my hand as we walked into a large teal and white building. It looked more like a warehouse than a church. There was no cross or steeple on top, and it was much larger than any church I'd ever visited.

Following Shaina into the sanctuary, my eyes widened in awe. Thousands of people filtered in and milled about, greeting each other warmly as the clock on the back wall drew close to 6:00 p.m. Taking a seat next to Shaina, I tried to wrap my mind around the excitement buzzing in the air. It was a level of stimulation I wasn't used to in church. Soon the pastor took the stage. With reddish hair and a charismatic smile, he greeted the congregation.

"Well, good evening, everyone! Isn't it great to be in the house of the Lord?"

He opened with prayer, his palms upward as he walked the stage back and forth. With a hearty "Amen!" the worship leader started in on a full band arrangement of "Shout to the Lord," inviting people to stand and sing.

I was both intrigued and fascinated. In the back of the room, a barefoot lady danced with a ribbon on a wand. In another corner, a gray-haired man shook a tambourine to the beat. Raised primarily in Nazarene churches prior to this, I had never experienced people worshiping in this charismatic pentecostal style. They had a contagious joy about them and seemed to be encountering God in a way that was real, authentic, and tangible. It ignited something fresh and alive inside me.

"Thank God, thank God, thank God," the pastor proclaimed as he took the stage again a full forty minutes later, following the offering. It was a phrase he was known for. He then proceeded to speak in a down-to-earth, relatable way that engaged me.

During my earlier years of Sunday school, I learned about Jesus from flannel boards, practiced Bible drills, and sang songs like "Give Me Oil in My Lamp" and "Father Abraham Had Many Sons." Although I felt a connection with Jesus from a young age, this church experience was different. It was no longer just stories from an ancient book; it was a way of engaging God and life that was alive and active. As a girl whose upbringing forced me to stifle, suppress, and compartmentalize my emotions, being in an environment that allowed the free expression of them felt liberating.

The relaxed Sunday-evening atmosphere gave the energy in the room a feeling of refreshment for the soul. It wasn't rushed. Rather, it provided space to slow down and breathe. And room to breathe is exactly what I found my heart needing more and more as I entered my teen years.

I returned with Shaina the next week, and the next. Before long, it was my new church home. I dutifully attended the Nazarene church with my family on Sunday mornings so that I could go to Centered Life with Shaina on Sunday nights. My parents weren't thrilled that I was attending two different churches, but they allowed it because they could see the life it sparked inside me.

Over the next three years, Centered Life became my home away from home. It was where I longed to be, often even more than my own house. My parents continued to encourage me to foster my "walk with the Lord" in our time together as a family, but Sunday night church was where I found my personal relationship with God flourishing. It was my safe place and, for the first time, a place where I could go without having to wear a mask of perfection. I didn't have to put on a show or be in the spotlight or known by who my mother was or what my father did; I didn't have to pretend that I had it all together or be constantly smiling or beaming with happiness; I could just be me. And I craved that. If home and with friends was where I had to play a role or perform a part, church and my worship time with God was where I got to just . . . *be*. I could be genuine, transparent, and real because it was just me and God. It was my safe haven. Those early years I spent at Centered Life are still some of the sweetest memories with God that I have. It laid a foundation for me that ended up carrying me through the years to come.

I don't know what my life would look like today if I hadn't had those years at Centered Life. In many ways it reinforced everything my parents wanted me to believe, but when I wasn't being taught how to think or act, the countless hours I spent filling journal after journal, pouring out my heart to God, were sacred. If all I knew of God were the legalistic rules and regulations that were the bedrock of my religious upbringing, it's quite possible that I would have left faith altogether once I came out as gay. But the time I spent as a teenager at Centered Life before realizing I was gay was time spent cultivating a deeply personal relationship with Jesus. And in many ways, I believe that is what saved my faith.

Wednesdays and Sundays were my favorite days of the week. Graduating from high school at just sixteen, I enrolled in a community college program to become a sign language interpreter. The college campus was just opposite Centered Life, and after class on Wednesdays I walked across the open field to the church. I spent my afternoons in the prayer center on the Centered Life campus. It was always peaceful. The attractive building featured a sanctuary with floor-to-ceiling windows that gave a breathtaking view of the Rocky Mountains. It was open and available for prayer 24/7, and a rotating schedule of people led worship during different time slots throughout the week. That's how I met Lena, the pianist who had such an influence on me as a teen. She led a two-hour worship slot every Wednesday afternoon.

Listening to her, I quickly fell in love with Lena's style. Leaning into that style for myself was like setting my fingers free. My music began to take a shape of its own and I began writing my own music and leading my own weekly slot at the prayer center. However, music wasn't the only way that Lena influenced me. While it was her musical style that drew me to her at first, as I got to know Lena I was also drawn to her authenticity. Much like her way of playing the piano, Lena didn't live by the rules. She was down-to-earth and practical, and she thrived on knowing God, having fun, and being true to herself all things that drew me to her. As a firstborn child, a people-pleaser, a role model, a daughter to prominent evangelical leaders, and someone whose parents thrived on the consistency rules provided, I was slowly suffocating inside. I desperately wanted to live freely without feeling like I was a human spotlight, always expected to be the shining example. Lena embodied that kind of freedom—she captivated and fascinated me all at once.

While it is easy to speculate that I simply had a crush on Lena, that was not the case. What I felt when I was with her wasn't a romantic attraction. Twenty years my senior, Lena was modeling the type of life I could only dream of. She was intentional, she was carefree and unencumbered by the legalism that my brand of religion required—and it was those traits that drew me to her.

There was one additional trait that Lena had, a hallmark that no one else in my life possessed: the ability to make me feel safe. Everywhere I went in life, I felt the need to smile through and hold things together. But with Lena, I was given permission to feel my emotions and process them openly. She validated my feelings when everyone else minimized them. When my parents downplayed how I was feeling or told me to "just pray and trust God more," Lena was the one who saw past my smile and acknowledged my pain. I had never felt so seen, protected, and safe.

Our relationship deepened into a mentorship even more when "just another day at church" took a turn for the worse and became an experience with religious trauma that would mark me for life. I was only sixteen when a mentally unstable, middle-aged man who was in town for a prophetic conference approached me at the prayer center, preying upon my innocence as a young, single female and taking advantage of my trusting nature. He claimed he had a "word from God" and began praying and "prophesying" things over me that were completely contrary to everything I knew to be true and, in hindsight, made no logical sense. His words and actions were creepy (in the most buttoned-up, spiritual sense of the word)—but it was more than that. Something about the way he touched me when he prayed for me made me feel violated and shook me to the core. I couldn't explain why, but I knew it deeply distorted my sense of safety. Deluded by the myth that everyone who claims to be a Christian is trustworthy, I lacked the wit and wisdom to set boundaries in a situation of uncertainty. I knew something felt off in my gut, but I was taught that my gut couldn't be trusted. Instead, I was told that my heart was deceitful (as stated in Jeremiah 17:9) and that I should submit to the "governing authorities" who have been "established by God" (as stated in Romans 13:1 NIV). So rather than listening to my own inner voice and speaking up or trying to leave the situation, I stood there frozen, shaking on the inside, but unable to say or do anything to advocate for myself.

I didn't want to be guilty of blocking the voice of God, so I let it continue. I didn't know that I had the right to speak up, because no one had taught me agency. I didn't know that simply *saying* you've heard from God doesn't give people the right to act however they please. I didn't know that I could walk away and leave, rather than stay captive in a spiritually and emotionally unsafe situation. *I didn't know.* I didn't know because no one taught me to trust my inner Knowing. I didn't know because no one told me that boundaries were healthy, even with people in authority. I didn't know because no one taught me that even *church* could be unsafe. Rather, I believed that those who were older than me (whether I knew them or not) had more experience, knowledge, and wisdom and that I should respect and heed their advice whenever God or religion was involved. I was taught that feelings can't be trusted, so we must rely on "truth." And I was taught that as a woman, I didn't know the truth, because I was not equal to men. The messages of inferiority were subtle, but clear. This culmination of things that I both *did* and *didn't* know cost me my safety in the one place I had always felt safe: church.

What happened to me that day was not only deeply inappropriate, it was deeply traumatic. It left me feeling violated. I struggled to understand why an encounter where nothing explicitly sexual happened could make me feel as if I'd been assaulted. Words to explain what happened eluded me, but I knew I was not okay. In the weeks that followed, my body began to mirror the level of violation that my soul had experienced. I became hypervigilant, paranoid, and on high alert wherever I went, especially at church. I experienced nightmares, frequent flashbacks, extreme anxiety, and panic attacks when anything even remotely resembled the situation. This continued for months and is where my experience with post-traumatic stress disorder (PTSD) first began.

This is the epitome of spiritual abuse. People in power abusing authority over people in their care are—at best—a baseline for why so many people are wounded by religion and leaving faith systems all together. The Southern Baptist Convention, the Catholic priests, the Ted Haggards and Jerry Falwell Jrs.—all public examples of private sexual encounters exposed. Yet how many encounters (like mine) go unexposed, unreported, and the perpetrators are not held accountable for their actions? How many other young people, women, people with disabilities, people of color, or LGBTQ+ people have stayed silent in moments of religious trauma or religious sexual abuse due to the power dynamic at play, the indoctrinated mistrust of self, and the lack of acquired agency? The extent of these violations, even with hashtags like #MeToo and #ChurchToo, is one that we'll never be able to fully measure.

For years I felt embarrassed and ashamed over what happened that night, like it was *my* fault—something *I* had done wrong. As a by-product of patriarchy, women have been conditioned to believe that we are responsible for any harm that may befall us. We've been told that if we feel violated, it's because we dressed too provocatively, our skirt was too short, our neckline too low, our makeup too heavy, or our smile too much to resist. Instead of being believed, we've been shamed. Such victim-blaming also happens to men who are sexually abused, just with different verbiage. In their case, they're too soft, too effeminate, too emotional, not strong enough, not brave enough, not manly enough. The damage is the same. Depreciated self-worth, pain, violation, and shame . . . often at the hands of faith leaders we've been told to trust.

No matter how hard I tried to brush it off, what happened that night ignited extreme fear in me and was the first in a series of incidents that taught me that church and its leaders aren't always safe.

Lena and I bonded deeply in the months following that encounter. With gentleness and patience, she walked me through the healing process. Her presence and words had an ability to disarm me and make me feel safe, which allowed space to not only counteract the lies that were spoken over me at the prayer center that night, but also mend some of the wounds from the perfectionistic training of my upbringing. Her authenticity, vulnerability, and transparency gently pulled my walls down. She could see the fear in my eyes, fear that I didn't know how to communicate, and she allowed me to be scared, to question, and to process without feeling the need to prescribe an instant fix. The victim of religious trauma herself, she had deep empathy for my pain. Her reminders that I was going to be okay grounded me and provided me comfort when I couldn't find it anywhere else.

I had been struggling for so long from being forced into a cookie cutter mold that didn't fit, having no safe outlet for my emotions and therefore suppressing them, and also (subconsciously) suppressing the beginnings of my struggle with sexuality. I tried hard to fit into the Christian carbon copy I was expected to fulfill, but I felt like an outlier everywhere I went.

Being homeschooled put me ahead of my peers in education, but it also kept me behind socially. I loved the benefit of accelerated learning—it kept me challenged and

engaged, which I needed. But the downside was that graduating from high school at the age of sixteen and having
my associate degree by eighteen made it hard for me to fit
in and make friends, especially friends my own age. I was
sixteen and attending community college, which meant I
didn't fit in with the high school crowd, but I also still lived
at home and was too young to fit in with the college crowd.
I was as mature as my college classmates, but the youngest
person in every class I joined. Often seen as the baby of the
group, I hated feeling patronized about my age. It served as
a constant reminder that I didn't *really* fit in.

I also didn't relate to my friends when it came to lik-
ing and dating boys.

"Isn't Jonathan Taylor Thomas so hot?" they'd ask me
as we looked at the poster of the teenage actor on their wall.

"Oh, I know!" I'd say, just to fit in. But in reality, I
felt nothing. It didn't interest me or make me feel anything
the way it clearly did for them. Now I can see that what
many of my friends felt for boys, I felt for many of my
female friends. Perhaps if I had known other gay people or
taken sex ed classes in school or simply been exposed to
life outside of evangelicalism, I would have had the words
to accompany my buried feelings. But because I lacked
the exposure and vocabulary to identify what was happening inside of me, these feelings (or lack thereof) didn't
make sense, and my lack of interest in the opposite sex
caused me to feel even more alienated. Unfortunately, it
would still be many years before I could finally put a name
to my struggles.

All I knew was, I was in pain. And at the age of sixteen, Lena was the first person in my life to ever tell me
it was okay to cry. With a lifetime of pent-up emotions, I
needed that permission desperately. Fear of what it would

look like to actually give voice to my emotions often petrified me. But Lena's patience, coupled with her ability to read between the lines and hear what I couldn't say, broke down my walls one by one. Without a doubt, that's why I felt safe with and trusted Lena so deeply. She met me where I was, and that's something no one had ever done for me before.

I'm so grateful I met Lena when I did, because not long after the traumatic incident at church, the lifetime of emotions I'd worked hard to conceal started leaking through the cracks and became evident in my mental health. With the stigma and shame that accompanied it, I knew I was going to need Lena's support to help me through.

Chapter 5

WHEN MENTAL HEALTH IS TABOO

It was a cold January day when what started as a routine trip to the library took a sharp turn. Scanning the holds shelf for my own book, I happened upon a book my mom had placed on hold: *Obsessive Compulsive Behaviors*. Opening to the table of contents out of anxious curiosity, I became uneasy the moment my eyes met the words "Trichotillomania" and "Hair-Pulling Disorder." A knot formed in the pit of my stomach. Reading further into the chapter, I saw myself described on the pages before me.

The book described trichotillomania (TTM) as a compulsive hair-pulling disorder with traits similar to obsessive-compulsive disorder (OCD). It said that the age of onset was typically between eleven and thirteen, and it can often be associated with a stressful event. While some outgrow it, for others it lasts for life. Symptoms include noticeable hair loss, low self-esteem, significant distress at social functions, and depression.

The book described something I'd been trying to conceal for years. I thought back, trying to pinpoint when this behavior first started. I remembered experiencing some OCD behaviors as a young child, but those faded as I grew older. The hair-pulling, however, started sometime not long before my thirteenth birthday, which fell right in line with the typical age of onset.

Pulling gave me a sense of calm when I was stressed, but it also made me loathe myself afterward. I'd look in the mirror at my patchy lashes and eyebrows and think to myself, "I am *so* ugly."

Often the pulling was subconscious, and I wouldn't even realize I was doing it until it was too late. Once I started, it was very hard to stop. I hated that I couldn't control it, and I hated that it made my struggles so visible. It was embarrassing, and as a result I pulled away from people and for years couldn't even look people in the eye. Making contact with someone's eyes allowed them to see mine. I didn't want anyone to see. I hid behind glasses and makeup, but it wasn't enough. If they didn't notice on sight, the discomfort I felt was displayed in my self-conscious mannerisms. I avoided swimming and trips to water parks with friends out of fear that my makeup might wash off and reveal my bald, patchy eyebrows. I dreaded playful make-overs, knowing that allowing someone that close to my face would reveal my missing lashes. This disorder eroded my confidence and made me extremely self-conscious about my appearance.

My perfectionist nature tried to hide and control my hair-pulling at any cost, but almost always left me discouraged at my lack of willpower. Not realizing the chemical and even genetic components until years later, I felt isolated in my struggle and did everything in my power to compartmentalize and hide it. Even in my private journal, I didn't feel safe enough to write "hair-pulling" on the pages. Instead, I used code words like "my bad habit" out of embarrassment and shame. I had no idea that this compulsive behavior that I couldn't control was a real medical condition with a name, and that many others (including some of my cousins) shared the same diagnosis.

I don't remember ever hearing mental health talked about in a positive way growing up. It was a taboo topic that came coupled with shame and humiliation. The lack of dialogue around mental health as part of holistic well-being affected the way those of us in evangelical culture saw one another and also the way we saw ourselves. Medical care was acceptable for physical ailments, but not emotional ones. Our unwillingness to see our mind like any other part of our body that may need support from doctors and medications is responsible for a great amount of unnecessary distress. It has caused conditions like depression, anxiety, bipolar disorder, and post-traumatic stress disorder (along with other conditions, like TTM) to go undiagnosed and untreated for years because religious people believed that God would heal them or that it was wrong to ask for help. LGBTQ+ people are already two times more likely to have a mental health disorder in their lifetime compared to straight men and women, and two and a half times more likely to experience depression, anxiety, or substance misuse.[1] Add the component of mental health being a taboo topic, and you have a recipe for disaster for those of us who grew up queer in the church.

At the time, I was completely convinced that TTM was the result of my own "sin." What that sin was, I couldn't tell you. Only that I was somehow deeply flawed, because regardless of countless attempts, I couldn't simply stop. I repented thousands of times, begging God for forgiveness and healing for a behavior I now realize wasn't at all due to lack of faith or a need to trust God more. Yet faith and trust were foundational tenets of what I was taught to believe. If there was an area where you were struggling, it was simply because you needed to try harder, pray more, and have more faith that God would heal you. When I did all that to no avail, I was left with no other option but to believe that there was either something wrong with me or I simply wasn't trying hard enough. Christians, especially those with a completely insulated upbringing like mine, weren't supposed to struggle—with anything. Not only did it indicate the status of your relationship with God, it also reflected on the reputation of your family. And for me and my family, the expectation was high.

Having a visible and diagnosable "struggle" felt like everything I was trained *not* to be, and also evidence that what I *was* trained to be was too heavy a burden to carry. Bessel van der Kolk's groundbreaking book *The Body Keeps the Score* explores the brain, mind, and body connection in the storing and healing of trauma. Based on decades of research and clinical practice, van der Kolk explains how "the terror and isolation at the core of trauma literally reshapes both brain and body,"[2] creating a physical manifestation of all that we endure emotionally. My body started "keeping the score" young. Oh, how I wish I had been given the proper support and tools as a teenager, rather than twenty years later when the score my body kept was significantly larger and coupled with the debilitating diagnoses of both rheumatoid arthritis and late-stage Lyme disease. TTM was just the beginning of what storing emotions and trauma in my body would cost me. Without the proper resources, and without a safe place to release fear and pain, far too many of us have faced the same fate.

Deep down, I felt relieved to finally have an explanation for this behavior that tormented me and stole my confidence. At the same time, the thought of having a medically diagnosable disorder was terrifying for someone expected to maintain a perfect persona. As estranged as I was from my emotions, I was surprised at the range of feelings that bubbled to the surface: shock at the discovery of this medical condition; anger that my mom knew about it and hadn't discussed it with me; fear of what this meant for the family image I was trying so hard to uphold; anxiety about what people would think of me if and when they found out. This was a part of me that no one knew, a part of me I didn't *want* anyone to know. To my knowledge, no one but my parents was aware of my hair-pulling. I had never told anyone. But now I needed to; I needed someone I could confide in and process this new information with.

Lena was the obvious choice. She was the only person with whom I felt safe enough to talk openly. I promised myself that no matter how hard or uncomfortable it was for me to expose this impulsive and embarrassing behavior, I would gather the needed courage to tell Lena at piano lessons the next day.

In the car on the way to Lena's house, my heart raced with anxiety and my knuckles turned white from my grip on the wheel. I hadn't determined exactly how I was going to tell her; all I knew was that I was about to share with her something I had never shared with anyone, and that required a lot of trust. I fought to keep my hands from shaking as I sat at the piano, but my anxiety was obvious. Seeing through my façade, Lena wrapped up my piano lesson early and took me into a back room for some privacy so we could talk.

I took a seat as Lena looked at me inquisitively, but fear of what she would think of me once I showed her what was behind my mask kept the words lodged in my throat. Finally, I simply took the library book out of my bag, opened to the correct page, and handed it to her.

Waiting for her to read and unable to hold back my tears any longer, I sat there and cried. I had no idea what the consequences were for allowing someone to see the real me; I just knew that I needed Lena. I couldn't afford to lose her, and I deeply hoped that this new information about a very tender piece of my heart wouldn't cause her love for me to change or disintegrate.

To this day, I can still see the look on her face and hear the tone in her voice when she responded. "Amber, look at me. This changes *nothing*. I love you very much," she insisted. "You have nothing to be ashamed of. You are beautiful, and I mean that. Whatever going through this looks like, I'll be by your side. I want you to let me know what I can do to help."

Her words quickly dispelled all my fears. I should have known that Lena would respond with love rather than judgment. Her outlook on life was different from my family's. She believed in being who you are and embracing where you are in life, rather than trying to measure up to who everybody wants you to be. She gave little regard to what others thought of her and instead focused her energy on being true to herself.

I, on the other hand, was supposed to represent my family and our reputation as a Focus family with poise and grace. Discovering I had TTM was like discovering a hole in my armor, and telling someone about it was revealing my weakness. I felt vulnerable and, knowing nothing other than the environment in which I was raised, feared the implications of trusting someone with the powerful knowledge that I wasn't as perfect as I appeared.

As I left that afternoon, an imprint was made on my heart that would last forever. For the first time, someone had seen the deepest parts of me and wasn't appalled. Lena changed my life that day. The permission she gave me to be flawed and human was so refreshing. I finally felt seen and safe at the same time. It was immensely healing for me. She provided a safety net to risk being authentic, and because of it, my worldview changed. For the first time, I learned to value honesty more than the mask.

My parents did everything they could think of in order to help me with pulling. My mom found Bible verses about strength and faith and wrote them out on index cards to place around my room. They prayed with me and for me. They designed an incentive chart with rewards if I didn't pull for certain lengths of time—which worked sometimes, but affected my self-esteem even more if I didn't measure up. I felt like I was disappointing them. They also made me wear socks over my hands at night so I wouldn't pull and put Vaseline on my fingertips, so they'd be too slippery to grip the hair. My mom even read somewhere that chocolate-covered raisins made it worse, so when the family was enjoying a sweet snack, she'd remind me that I couldn't have any because they didn't want it to make my pulling any worse. It was degrading and hurtful to be singled out, but I complied. Yet it rarely produced results.

Once my hair-pulling behavior was labeled as TTM, my parents did seek outside help. They took me to a psychiatrist who coldly asked me about my behaviors and stress. They also took me to a "Christian counselor," which meant that the advice given in therapy would be congruent with the religious tenets that were practiced in my household. Therapy in any form held great stigma because needing counseling was already a sign of weakness—a sign that something was wrong—and good Christians who had Jesus weren't supposed to have anything wrong. But the negative connotation of having a mental health disorder exceeded the stigma of counseling. So my parents found a Christian therapist who was knowledgeable in TTM. Our conversations were awkward and felt like part of a formula to simply "cure" me. I didn't trust her and therefore simply gave her the answers she was looking for, not how I really felt. I was smart and knew how to play the game. I'd been trained all my life for this. Nobody would know anything I didn't want them to know. I was the expert masker. *I. was. fine.* Only I wasn't and I knew it. But I also knew that I needed to talk to someone who made me feel safe. Someone like Lena. Being forced to meet with a counselor whose only mission was to return me to packaged perfection, I decided the best route was to tell the therapist what she wanted to hear so I could get my ticket out of this weekly meeting with obligatory vulnerability.

When all those efforts failed and I was still pulling consistently, my parents resorted to taking me to see one of our church pastors who specialized in deliverance ministry. These meetings took place during the week, off-site in his private office. After I arrived with both my parents one afternoon, a tall, husky man and his wife prepared me for exorcism. They laid their hands on me, begged God to come, and began calling out my demons of depression, anxiety, and hair-pulling. It was extremely unsettling, even terrifying. The pastor spoke with authority in a loud voice:

"Lift your hands upward, Amber."

"Believe in the power of Jesus, Amber!"

"Proclaim that you want to be free, Amber!!"

"Denounce the power these demons have over your life, Amber!!!"

"I rebuke you, spirit of depression, and command that you come out so that Amber can be free in the name of Jesus!"

It's experiences like these that cause me to realize just how far we have *not* evolved. Superstitions and lack of knowledge and understanding around medicine in the 1600s and 1700s caused women who believed in the healing power of herbs to be labeled witches and burned alive. Children who got sick were called demon-possessed and left for dead. Weak babies whose parents believed them to be changelings were left outside for the fairies. As archaic as these notions sound today, the reality is that my experience with exorcism—and the experiences of so many others from charismatic, pentecostal, or evangelical backgrounds—is not much evolved from these superstitious practices. They're rooted in ignorance and fear yet perpetuate real and lasting harm.

In situations like mine, rather than taking into account the chemical and medical components involved in conditions such as TTM (not to mention the effects of trauma), there's a deep desire and need to fix it or make it go away. If nothing you've tried has worked, then it must be because unseen demonic forces are at work and you need to be delivered from them. These beliefs have caused additional layers of complex religious trauma for many—especially those with physical or mental disabilities. It's also an ableist mind-set that says, "Because you differ from what I perceive as normal, we need to fix you." This is why it is imperative that we continue to fight for education around diversity and inclusion, mental health awareness as part of whole-body health, and holistic care. If we can lessen the stigma around mental health, especially in faith spaces, we have the potential to also lessen instances of religious trauma that come as a result of people believing that they need to be delivered from dark or demonic forces.

Having demons cast out of you at the age of sixteen is scarring and traumatic. And much like the instance I experienced with that strange man at the prayer center, I felt trapped between being open to God, as I'd been taught, and feeling afraid and unsafe.

I managed to hold myself together for the length of the session that day, but once my deliverance session was over, my parents realized that nothing, not even an exorcism, could cure me. They were getting discouraged.

One of the only memories I have of my dad losing his temper was over the issue of my hair-pulling. Standing in the kitchen late one night, his patience with my lack of recovery was spent and he exploded.

"Can't you stop?!? Why don't you just stop!? Can't you see how horrible you look? Just look at yourself in the mirror! You look awful!" This was the first time I'd experienced such an outburst from my dad. His words stung, hurt, and rang in my head for years to come. Of course I wanted to stop. Didn't he know that? I was riddled with shame and disappointment and wanted nothing more than for this compulsion to go away—but I was powerless to control it.

Knowing that I was disappointing my parents caused me to distance. Like many teens who struggle with their parents, I looked to other adults for support and advice. FOTF taught that positive role models for your kids are important, and my parents believed that mentoring from other Christian adults was both helpful and healthy. But it was bittersweet for them as I grew closer to Shaina and Lena. It was hard for my mom to see me confiding in her friends rather than in her. Yet no matter how many times I tried to explain to her how their reactions minimized the way I felt, it always seemed to fall on deaf ears.

In hindsight, I believe my parents wanted to help me but didn't know how. At times, I think it frightened them. The things I struggled with didn't add up for a girl with my homeschooled, Focus on the Family, Christian upbringing. My parents followed all the models, they read all the books, they raised me with all the principles and values that FOTF and James Dobson encouraged. They couldn't understand where all this was coming from. So, like any good Christian parent, they tried to push me closer to Jesus.

Our reputation as a family grew during my teen years as my dad's work at FOTF continued to expand and flourish. *Adventures in Odyssey* reached a global audience as they continually released new episodes, and a new radio drama for adults called *Radio Theatre* was created. To avoid a similarity in sound between the two, *Adventures in Odyssey* continued to be recorded with actors in Los Angeles while *Radio Theatre* took up its recording sessions with actors in London, England. This project required quite a bit of travel on my father's part but received acclaim early on when one of the first dramas they produced, on the life of Dietrich Bonhoeffer, won a Peabody Award.

I was proud of my father's work, but struggled with feeling as though I was always living in the shadow of my family. At FOTF, I was Dave Arnold's daughter; with the Green Gable Girls, I was my mother's daughter; and as my brother got older, he became quite popular at Centered Life, so I was known as his sister. I was always identified by my relation to someone else in my family.

Years after my brother moved out of state and I moved to Denver, I decided to visit a church plant of Centered Life in the Denver area. Hoping no one would recognize me, I slipped in just before the service started and sat in the back. I wanted to be somewhere familiar, but I also wanted to be invisible. After worship, we were told to greet those around us. I turned to *one* person and shook their hand, and they looked at me and said, "Hey, you're Daniel's sister, aren't you?"

I exhaled in defeat.

"Yes, I am," I said with a forced smile. But I was frustrated. Situations like this made me feel invisible and unable to be seen for who I was apart from my family. Because of this, I often just wore a smile and took on the problems of others without any safe place to share my own. Lena was really my only confidante.

But then one day, my very worst fear came true.

Lena and I had just finished another heart-to-heart conversation in the hall after church one night. True to form, she made me feel heard, validated, and safe. Always grateful for the way she made time for me, I gave her a hug as we went to leave, and said, "Thanks for taking the time to talk, Lena. It really means a lot to me."

"You're worth every minute of it, Amber," she replied. "I love you very much!" And with that, she turned and left.

I had no idea that something snapped inside Lena that night. The next day, she contacted my parents, came to our home, and returned the money they had paid for my piano lessons that month. Then, without even a hug goodbye, she walked out the door, never to speak to me again.

I was shell-shocked. I kept replaying the situation over and over in my mind. Nothing was wrong when we parted the night before. Everything seemed fine. What the hell happened!?! I couldn't make sense of it. Countless times over the previous few years, I'd asked her if our talks together were getting to be too much. Each time, she had replied, "No, not at all!" If that were true, then why would she so unexpectedly abandon me? She knew how much our relationship and time together meant to me. She knew how much I looked up to her, how much I needed her. It felt like the ultimate betrayal from the only safe person I had. I was devastated. I was perplexed, confused, and scared, but I was also deeply hurt. Lena promised that she would always be there when I needed her, that she loved me, and that she would stick by me no matter what. Now, overnight, she was gone. In an instant, she had erased herself from my life. Even when I saw her at church, she didn't acknowledge me. I was suddenly invisible.

To this day, the only thing that makes sense to me is that she neglected to tell me how she really felt, and in fact *was* overwhelmed by the weight of what I shared. Perhaps knowing I wasn't able to trust my parents with the same depth of information, she suddenly became frightened by the responsibility (I was still a minor) and it caused her to pull away. Today, I can understand how she may have felt that way. The things I confided in her weren't easy. But it still hurts to think of how she handled it. I wish she had been honest with me when I asked her. I deserved to know and have some warning. She was the person I trusted most, the only one who truly made me feel safe, the only one with whom I didn't have to wear a mask—the only one who would let me cry.

In time, my pain turned to anger, and I decided that if the one person I had finally trusted with my heart was capable of walking out on me, then I wasn't going to trust *anybody*. I completely shut down my emotions. I closed the vault to my heart and locked it tight. I decided I would handle things on my own from now on, and did whatever I could to numb the pain.

*One night, in the midst of unbearable heartache and not knowing what else to do, I picked up a shaving razor,

---

*Trigger warning: Please keep yourself safe and skip this paragraph if you feel that reading about self-injury may trigger you.

uncovered my right leg, and sliced it across the skin of my upper thigh. It drew blood and I experienced an odd sense of release. It was as if all the pent-up emotions I'd harbored inside spilled out of me with the blood. I felt both temporarily numb from my emotional pain and temporarily free from it. The physical pain on my body was somehow easier than the emotional pain in my heart. It was tangible and I could control it. It was symbolic of what I felt inside—an outward representation of my inner pain. Over time, the blade became my new friend, my secret way of coping. It was never a cry for help; rather, it was my way of surviving the quiet inner agony my heart was bearing. And I shared it with no one.

Chapter 6

DEFYING GENDER NORMS AND SOCIAL EXPECTATIONS

Whether by nature or by nurture, I was a girlie girl in my youth and fit the prescribed gender norms to perfection. I enjoyed dolls, tea parties, makeup, and playing dress-up. I often wore dresses and never liked jeans. They were too restricting. Belts were also out of the question. I preferred what I then called stretch pants (because we didn't believe in yoga). But as I got into my teens, no matter what I was wearing, I never felt comfortable about my appearance (especially with the effects of my TTM) and felt like I constantly struggled to measure up to society's standards.

One day, I saw a pair of carpenter jeans in the men's department that looked comfortable. Similar to the hoodie selection that still occupies a large portion of my wardrobe, it felt like a piece of clothing I could put on, wrap myself up in, and hide inside.

I bought the carpenter jeans and started wearing them. A lot. Since this was a notable change to my family, my dad decided to comment.

"What's up with those jeans, Amber? What are you, a cross-dresser?" he said with a smirk, half sarcastic, half serious. I shrugged it off with a forced smile, trying to hide how much it hurt.

"What size are they anyway?" he continued, seeing how loose they were. When I told him, he laughed, implying that the size was bigger than anything *he'd* ever bought. I tried not to show how much his comments dented my self-esteem. This wasn't the first time I'd heard one of my family members make a condescending remark about LGBTQ+ people, but even though I didn't yet identify as gay, this comment stung because it was personal. I already felt uneasy in my own skin. His snide comments made it clear that I should be both thinner and more feminine. It was another lesson that, in my family, it was unsafe to be myself.

*Trying to shield myself from further condescending comments and stung by the loss of Lena, I remained alone in my pain and continued to turn to self-injury to soothe myself. Like a friend you keep going back to for comfort, even when you know they're bad for you, I knew cutting wasn't healthy. But out of all my coping mechanisms, this one brought the most relief.

*They were mostly surface cuts at first. But like many negative coping behaviors, self-injury took a little more each time to get the same release—more cuts, bigger cuts, longer cuts, deeper cuts. Soon both my thighs were completely covered in long, thin slice marks. Although I tried to save cutting as a last resort, when I did give in, each cut had to exceed the last. Relying on my polished poker face to cover my pain with a smile, I knew how to keep my cuts hidden so that no one ever saw them. Showcasing my weaknesses made me feel defeated and vulnerable—like I wasn't strong enough. I hated not feeling strong enough. So I once again found a way to hide my pain by wearing knee-length shorts, swimsuits with skirts, and later, long-sleeved shirts and hoodies.

---

*Trigger warning:** Please keep yourself safe and skip this paragraph if you feel that reading about self-injury may trigger you.

*I've heard from a lot of people who felt completely shocked by the suicide of hip-hop dancer Stephen "tWitch" Boss in 2022. Just like when we lost comedic actor Robin Williams in 2014, people commented, "I didn't see this coming; he always looked so happy."

It's important to remember that smiles don't always convey happiness. Sometimes they are used to cover up pain. It's a coping mechanism, a way of survival. Coping mechanisms—especially those used to meet society's expectations around happiness—are often passed down generationally. This is particularly pervasive in evangelical Christian homes. Smiles and laughter are also a way to break away from the pain, no matter how short or how brief. The weight of an unwanted pedestal and unmet expectations can be suffocating. Often, it's those who smile the biggest who are battling the deepest heartache. It's easy for the darkness to build over time. This is something that I knew well even as a teenager.

Deep inside I longed for someone to hear what I didn't know how to say. I longed for someone to see past my smile and tell me that I was safe. I longed for someone to be strong *for* me, so that I didn't have to always be strong for myself. I longed for someone like Lena. But instead, I was surrounded by superficiality. When I told someone how I was doing, I would often get a cliché response like, "Well, God will work everything out. Just believe, and good will come from this someday, you'll see."

Or, even worse, "Well, I'm glad you're doing well!" which always perplexed me after sharing something that left me feeling vulnerable or exposed. I've learned over time that these comments often come from people with privilege—those to whom difficulty is foreign and uncomfortable. Their comments had nothing to do with me and everything to do with them trying to ease the discomfort they were feeling.

Capitalism also contributes to this expectation of happiness as standard. Continually adding products to the market designed to make you thinner, happier, more youthful, less depressed, more fit, less anxious, more energetic, and so on, creates an inner dissatisfaction that convinces us we must have that next best thing in order to be what society deems "happy." Yet it's never enough. Not only that, but the deeper messaging conveys that *we* are never enough. And that is much more dangerous.

For me, the lack of empathy I received from those whom I needed to care caused me to retract and isolate my heart from people even further, making authenticity an even rarer occurrence. It felt like confirmation that feelings can't be shared and held safely with others.

One night, I finally leveled with myself and wrote out the fears I was feeling. As I looked at the page, I saw secrets I didn't even realize I was harboring inside:

I'm afraid that God is disappointed in me.
I'm afraid that nobody is who they claim to be.
I'm afraid to need people.
I'm afraid that nothing good lasts.
Sometimes I wonder why I've never been on a date.
I still want to self-harm and am ashamed because of it.
I go through the drive-through and then sit and eat
    in my car so people won't know that I'm lonely.
    Sometimes, I even convince myself.
I'm afraid that I may never be good enough.
I'm afraid to write down my secrets because admitting
    them on paper is proof that I've failed to live up to
    the expectations of others, myself, and God.

Bringing my own fears into the light, I could see that my pain was festering. With hope that it would provide the support I needed, I enrolled in The Fire, an internship program that Centered Life offered for young adults. It was a fifteen-hour-a-week program designed for leadership development, discipleship, and prayer.

The expectations in the program were high. They had a no-tolerance policy for smoking, alcohol, drugs, sex, "homosexuality," cursing, or—for the first semester—even dating. The list of things that we "Must Do" and "Must Not Do" was extensive, and we had to signify our agreement by signing a covenant of commitment to these standards for the next nine months—like Christian boot camp.

There was a long list of requirements to be a part of this internship: three two-hour prayer meetings a week, at least one weekly church service, a weekly gathering for everyone in The Fire, weekly accountability groups, cards to fill out attesting to whether you followed all the rules that week, and a standard of excellence in everything you did. As an adult, I look back at the list of obligations and find it ludicrous, even cultlike. But at the time, we were told we were radicals for Jesus. The leadership was strict about accountability and convinced us that seeking God while in this program was the only thing that mattered because we were the world-changers of the next generation. And in evangelical culture at that time, buzzwords like "passionate desperation," "zeal," and "on fire for God" were admirable qualities.

Not for the faint of heart, these internships were for the best, most committed type of Christ-followers. Growing up entrenched in this Christian culture, I was used to sacrifice and maintaining good appearances, so naturally I wanted to be among those who were in the elite club of "God's favorites."

But I was also in search of healing. Spending intentionally carved-out time to be present and engage with God gave me the much-needed space I longed for to just be. Apart from the more harmful messages that were being taught in the program in regard to who you were required to be and how you were required to live in order to earn God's favor, I found ways of my own that felt comfortable and safe (apart from the group) to be alone with just God and my journal. I worked hard to learn better boundaries, to resist taking on other people's baggage, and to trust the right people with my own. I explored what it meant to stand up for myself so that people couldn't take advantage of me. I fought for my dignity and worth.

I also educated myself about post-traumatic stress disorder (PTSD). Through my research, I learned that trauma physically alters your brain, making it unable to differentiate between past and present experiences. It leaves an imprint on your neural pathways, making it difficult to regulate fear and anxiety in situations that are not related (or only remotely related) to the actual trauma. With PTSD, even though the current situation may be totally different from the trauma, it acts like a mirror, flashing you back to that moment with the same intensity as when it initially took place, and causing you to believe that it's happening all over again.

For some trauma survivors, the fight-or-flight mode often has a third component: freeze. That's what I do. I freeze up while trauma wages war in my mind. Because I have PTSD and I'm an internal processor, there are times when I run the whole cycle of PTSD in my body and mind without anyone ever knowing or actually seeing an external clue, like a shackling fear that keeps me captive and silenced. I became so accustomed to my plastered-on Barbie-doll smile that I was able to hide my PTSD well. Living with this condition as a persistent real possibility and knowing that it could affect me and be completely unnoticed by the public eye was—and still can be—isolating, frightening, and at times debilitating. Retraining my brain as best as I could and becoming aware of my triggers helped me feel more grounded.

This new knowledge coupled with the alone time I spent with my journal and music before God brought me leaps and bounds in my process of healing. Slowly, the icy numbness in my heart melted, and I began to feel again. I started sleeping better, feeling more whole, and ceasing my coping mechanism of self-harm. I was happy, and I felt free. For the first time in several years, the clouds were clearing and the sun was shining through.

Completing The Fire was monumental for me. I felt as though I accomplished something greater than a degree or diploma that year. I accomplished the task of facing my fears, and found a great deal of healing and wholeness in return.

After graduating from The Fire, I worked in several temp positions at FOTF while my sign language interpreting job at the school was on summer break. Although I did go through an interview to get the temp jobs, my dad's reputation and work history there made it more protocol than an actual screening process. A friend of mine told me that when she interviewed at FOTF, they asked her five questions. The first three were about her relationship with God, and the other two were "What is your stance on abortion?" and "What is your stance on homosexuality?" Your response to those two questions informed them whether your priorities aligned with theirs.[1]

FOTF was a very traditional workplace. As a woman, I was required to wear skirts or dresses with pantyhose. This again enforced gender norms around how women were supposed to look and act feminine. It wasn't until 2009 that the new president, Jim Daly, instated a new dress code that allowed women to start wearing pants and men to stop wearing ties.[2] In addition to the dress code, daily time spent reading the Bible and praying were encouraged at home and required at work. We gathered by department for devotions and prayer each morning before the workday began, and a mandatory chapel service for the entire company was held once a month.

Despite their conservative policies, they wanted to be on the cutting edge of teen culture. So occasionally, on top of releasing articles about being successful in school or developing a relationship with God, they also featured articles focused on self-esteem, eating disorders, and even self-injury. However, as I began to do my own research, I found very little in the broader Christian culture that addressed some of these more difficult topics. It was as if topics like these were too dark for "real Christians" to struggle with and should be exclusive to what we called "the secular world" (or those without our brand of faith). But, as I could personally attest, they weren't. Self-injury was quickly becoming a coping mechanism similar to eating disorders in both religious and nonreligious environments. I knew from experience that Christian teens needed someone they could talk to without the stigma of not measuring up or having enough faith.

That's how my passion to reach young women like me began. By this time, I was over two years cut-free and I wanted to find a way to reach those who still suffered in silence. I wanted to obliterate the need for masks of perfection to even exist. I began actively pursuing my dream of using my experience to help other young girls when it came to the more taboo topics in the church: depression, anxiety, sexual abuse, trauma, and self-injury.

While focusing on self-injury was my passion, I wanted to help create a bridge of conversation for all these difficult topics. Today there are so many more resources available on these issues than there were back then. At that time there was next to nothing offering guidance out of self-harm from a Christian perspective, and I wanted to change that. I began sharing my story with others.

Several departments at FOTF invited me to talk during their devotional hour. The first time was to a group of fifty people. I was nervous to be so vulnerable with people who knew my family so well. I spotted my dad in the audience. He was proud of me for taking this step, but I knew some of the things I planned to say weren't going to be easy for him to hear. Sensitive to the fact that what I shared could reflect on him as a parent, I teetered between apprehension and determination to make a difference.

For twenty-five minutes, I shared my story and battle with self-injury, I talked about what I wanted to do to help others, and I gave them practical tips on why people self-injure as well as common signs to look for. At the end of my talk, everyone applauded my perseverance and thanked me for having the courage to share. Although it was a sensitive topic, they saw it as a victory story. I had overcome self-injury and was now a walking testimony for others.

I then spoke to several other departments at Focus, and talk of my story drifted through the campus. Someone from the media department heard what I was doing and contacted me about doing a TV spot for them on overcoming self-injury. When I agreed, they scheduled a camera crew to come to my apartment and film the spot. They interviewed me, asked some questions about my journey, and shot some footage of things I found therapeutic, like journaling. Soon I became the poster child for teens who have struggled with self-injury in the past but have now found "victory in Christ."

Although I no longer lived in my parents' house, we kept in touch often. For the several summers that I worked in temp positions at FOTF, my dad and I ate lunch together frequently. On Fridays, the whole family gathered at my parents' house for movies and pizza. While our relationship was superficial in matters of emotion and experience, it was also rich in love, tradition, and devotion to one another.

My mom and I continued to spend girl time together on a regular basis. We'd spend time scrapbooking or watching our favorite show. Seeing a creative wedding idea in a magazine, we'd dream about my future husband and family. Occasionally, she'd start a sentence with "One day when you have kids of your own. . . ." These topics allowed us to connect and relate to each other, even though how we felt about things was usually ignored.

I longed for a husband and family, and I still wore my purity ring with pride. But my heart was growing lonely in a way I hadn't felt before. Nevertheless, I still believed that if I followed God's will, in due time, I would be rewarded with the man of my dreams.

I know it pained my parents to see the struggles I'd gone through, yet they were always good about making a point to tell me how proud they were of my accomplishments. They especially loved that I was actively involved at church, both musically and spiritually. In their eyes, it was much better than what many other teens my age were doing. They also wholeheartedly supported it because being at church not only cultivated my relationship with God, but it also kept me inside the safe bubble of Christianity. Or so we all thought.

PART 2

SEXUALITY AND SHAME

Chapter 7
FATAL ATTRACTION

For the first twenty years of my life, it was not uncommon for my parents or other mentors to comment about my natural stage presence, how my smile radiated joy, or the idea that "God had big plans for my life."

It's ironic to me how some things can be completely turned on their head and yet still be true.

If someone had told me twenty years ago that I'd one day be writing books that would dismantle systems of oppression and advocate for LGBTQ+ inclusion in faith spaces, I would have raised my right eyebrow and given them a look that strongly conveyed, "Yeah, right." With an upbringing that taught me that the LGBTQ+ community was the archenemy of Christianity, responsible for destroying the family unit and America as we knew it, being part of that community was the furthest thing from my mind. In the minds of those who made those comments, doing big things for God certainly did *not* include work in LGBTQ+ advocacy. Yet with the journey I've taken and the experiences I've encountered, I believe the work of the Spirit is exactly that—to bring justice to the marginalized, to dismantle systems of oppression, to help others see beauty in diversity, and to fight for the equity, equality, and inclusion of all people. *Is that not the work of God?*

This version of walking out my faith was the furthest thing from my mind in my late teens and early twenties. I was a good girl, a people pleaser, a goal achiever, a dream chaser. I never dreamed that I would break all the rules and live outside of the box completely. That was for rebels.

But then something changed. I met a young woman through a mutual friend online. Like me, Brooke had been through a lot in her young life and also dealt with self-injury. I began encouraging and supporting her in her journey, and before long, Brooke planned a trip to visit me in order to consider joining The Fire internship at Centered Life. I was excited to connect with someone who had so many parallel experiences. But I *never* expected the turn my life was about to take because of it.

Brooke and I bonded instantly. So, when she applied and was accepted into The Fire, she asked if she could live with me, and I said yes.

I felt compassion and empathy for her as one who also battled self-harm. I hoped that with my experience and passion for helping others who dealt with self-injury, I could make a difference in her life. But we also hit it off well. Spending time together doing things that young adults do, we quickly became best friends. Whether we were shopping, sharing popcorn over movies, or having picnics at the park, the time we spent was full of making memories in simple moments. Laughter and lighthearted fun were balanced with deeper conversations around our shared experiences of trauma that led to self-harm. Since she was in The Fire, and I was still very active at church, much of our free time (whether at home or at church) was spent together. After feeling so isolated in my own journey and experience, it felt good to spend time with a friend who understood.

Brooke was nineteen when she came to live with me, and even though we were fast friends, I (being a few years older) also tried to be a mentor and positive role model for her. That was, of course, what I felt God was calling me to do—support girls who had similar struggles and experiences. In this case, I wanted to help Brooke heal from her past and find her way to wholeness. So, I listened to her, encouraged her, and supported her in whatever ways I could.

There is an understanding among evangelicals that if you believe God has called you to something, failing isn't an option. Failing implies weakness or an error in discernment. If we were doing things right, then our lives would be used to help others. We were expected to sacrifice our needs "for the sake of the call." Seeing my support for Brooke as an "assignment from God," healthy boundaries fell by the wayside.

Over time, between supporting her in her recovery and having fun as roommates and friends, the relational lines became blurred. Instinctively, I knew there was something unusual about the nature of our relationship, though I wasn't sure what. I just knew that it didn't fit within the confines of that little box we Christians were expected to live inside. Meanwhile, lack of dating experience and—let's be honest, lack of *life* experience—kept me naive and oblivious to the fact that other bonds were forming between us. Even though I knew deep down that most friends didn't do things like cuddle or hold hands, it felt easy and natural somehow. I liked how happy it made me, and feeling connected to Brooke in that way made me feel good. Since I couldn't quite pinpoint what was happening, I did what I was good at: compartmentalizing. I convinced myself that we were just close friends who had a special bond. *What else could it be?*

My own innocence kept me from recognizing the obvious, and because of that, I was completely unprepared for what happened next.

It was a Tuesday afternoon and we were lying on the bed in Brooke's room having a heart-to-heart conversation. After Brooke shared her current struggles, I reminded her again that she was safe in my home, that I loved her very much, and that I wasn't going anywhere. In fact, my words to Brooke probably sounded very much to her the way Lena's words once sounded to me: comforting, protective, safe. I remembered how much Lena's willingness to listen meant to me and wanted to provide the same opportunity for Brooke. I promised myself that I would never walk out on Brooke the way Lena had walked out on me. No matter how hard it got, I was determined to remain a faithful ally and supporter in her life. But because I failed to set more appropriate boundaries early on, within the safety of our heart-to-heart conversation that day, the unspeakable happened.

Suddenly, the tone of the conversation shifted. Affection gave way to a different emotion, one that stirred beneath the surface. Moving in closer, Brooke looked deep into my eyes. With a look of longing different from that of just close friends, she leaned into me until her lips gently touched mine with a sensual kiss.

I froze. It lasted only a moment, but it was a defining moment. *I had just kissed a girl.* Quickly backing away, we looked at each other wide-eyed and silent, in shock over what had just taken place. My head was spinning (in more ways than one). This was the first kiss I had shared with anyone, ever. But this was *not* how or with whom it was supposed to happen. I tried to stay in control. Brooke seemed to do the same. I couldn't tell if she was truly shocked the

way I was, or if she only pretended to be and had secretly
been thinking about this for some time. Either way, I knew
this couldn't be happening. Or shouldn't be.

Overcome by distress, I felt the unfortunate need to
talk to my college pastor and ask for guidance. I was confused about what was happening between us, but knew that
since Brooke was in The Fire and I was trying hard to mentor and support her through her recovery from self-injury,
kissing definitely was *not* appropriate, not to mention the
fact that we were both female! Since my options for coach-
ing and advice were limited at the time, Pastor Sharon
seemed like my best option. Sitting in her office, I listened
to the clock on the wall tick as I waited. It was about half the
speed of my nervous heartbeat. Finally, the door across the
room opened and she walked in.

"Hey, Amber, how's it going?" she said with a smile
as she took a seat in the black office chair near her desk.

Notorious for appearing much calmer and more put
together than I actually feel inside, I returned the smile and
replied, "I'm fine, thanks. How are you?"

Struggling to get to the reason for my visit, I began
explaining to Sharon the series of events that had led me
to her office. Trying to justify my actions and choices, I
carefully laid the foundation to make sure Sharon would
understand why Brooke came to live with me and what
my intentions were in having her as my roommate. I didn't
want to appear as messed up as I felt. I decided that this was
the tactful way to approach the situation.

Finally, I told her about the kiss, but was quick
to assure her that it had only happened once and that
Brooke and I had talked about it in detail and were sure
that if we simply established clearer boundaries, we could
move forward in a healthy manner. All I needed was for

Sharon to validate my already well-thought-out (and very in-control) plan.

That's not what happened.

"Amber, because I care about you, I need to speak the truth to you in love. This relationship isn't healthy. You talk about the two of you like you're a couple," she said with a serious tone. "She needs to move out immediately."

Move out?! I felt so misunderstood. I wasn't *in love* with Brooke. It had only happened once! It was a mistake! I was *in control!* Anger and frustration surfaced as I left, feeling even more confused and discouraged than when I walked in. I wanted to guide the conversation, to convince Sharon that the incident was no big deal. I wanted her to understand my intentions and be empathetic. I wanted her to agree that this could be resolved. I wanted her to believe in me.

But instead, Sharon tainted my first experience with love by dousing it in shame. Rather than encouraging me to explore my feelings and lending clarity to what had happened as a natural response to chemistry and connection, she drew distinct lines around what qualified as healthy love—and what happened between me and Brooke did *not* fit in that box. How different my experience could have been if she had celebrated my first romantic connection with another human being and normalized it as beautiful and holy and right. Instead, I was guilted into submission, once again tainting any sexual experience (but especially *that* experience) as disgusting and dirty. It reinforced my already well-ingrained expectations to turn off my feelings, shut down my desire, and let go of the one connection that was bringing me joy.

I look back at this now and think, *it was a kiss. A simple kiss.* But it wasn't. Because this kiss led to a suspicion

about a behavior linked to a belief system that was antitheti-
cal to everything we as evangelicals (and as an FOTF family) stood for and believed.

What I feared the most is exactly what happened.
My mistake was considered a sin by my pastor. And not
just any sin, but the worst kind of sin: homosexual sin.*
Brooke and I were now seen as dirty, tainted, and stained.
As much as I hated feeling misunderstood, I hated this
judgment even more. It was as if that one kiss now defined
us as "struggling homosexuals" in Sharon's eyes. That
messed with my desire to maintain appearances. My image
of perfection was tarnished.

And even more infuriating than the conversation
itself was that Sharon then spoke with one of Brooke's
mentors at The Fire about what had happened. Trust was
broken, and shame was used from both sides to control our
behavior and choices and coerce us into complying with
their demands. It was as if things said in confidence were
only kept in confidence to the degree that the person in
leadership felt comfortable. Once it crossed the line into
something difficult or sticky—something that was more
shades of gray than black-and-white—they felt they had
the right to disclose it to someone else to ease their con-
science and measure of responsibility. Repeatedly disappointed by people who claimed to be leaders of the faith, I
began to distance myself, both from church and from those
in church leadership.

The only positive advice we received came from
Brooke's therapist back home. She told Brooke not to

---

*The term "homosexual" is one that I no longer use in my vocabulary as I've found it to
only have negative connotations for myself and my queer siblings. However, I use it in
this context to exemplify how it has been used by Christians to form messages of guilt
and shame toward queer relationships that have resulted in religious trauma for so many.

run from the situation, but to stay and work it out. I was relieved. Finally, some sound advice that resonated with what my heart was telling me to do. We talked, we established boundaries, and I distanced myself emotionally to keep from blurring the lines. I was determined to make this work.

But despite my attempt at willpower, it wasn't long before that willpower gave way to chemistry and pent-up emotion, and we kissed again. The kiss was longer this time, more intimate; not passionate, but slow and sensual. Those few moments were so beautiful and amazing that I didn't want to let them go. I'd never felt anything like it. My whole body came alive, and I experienced a type of love I'd never felt before. In shock the first time we kissed, I had denied myself that pleasure the first time around. But this time, kissing Brooke brought a deep, inner joy I'd never known.

Then came the guilt. I knew that I shouldn't feel this way, no matter how beautiful it seemed—at least not with Brooke. Kissing another woman was strictly forbidden. Not only that, but I was supposed to be Brooke's role model. Although I didn't initiate the intimacy, I also felt powerless to stop it. I didn't know what to do. My mind and heart contradicted each other, and I was unsure which to follow. Confusion and conflict worked their way through my body, mind, and soul.

In the coming weeks, we both realized what we had been trying so hard to deny—there was a deeper connection and love present than that of just friends. Our relationship began to shift. We struggled in turmoil over the complexity of the situation. We couldn't deny the chemistry forming between us, but we couldn't escape the shame either. Guilt haunted our relationship. Yet, when we gave in to our obvious connection, there were moments of pure joy and love unlike anything either of us had ever experienced.

"How can something that feels so right be wrong?" we asked over and over together. It just didn't make sense. When we were together, we were so happy. How could happiness be bad? During this time, my joy was so evident that my dad even commented, saying I looked happier now than he'd seen me in a long time. *Gulp.* I couldn't deny it. I was definitely happy, but this time I knew it wasn't because of something that would make him proud.

Kissing led to experimenting, which led to more than kissing. It started to awaken things in me that my sheltered body didn't even know existed. Up until then, the sexual nature of my body had been quite foreign to me. I felt cheated in that way, as if my body had been hiding facts about my sexuality that were common knowledge to those around me. Now, new things were coming alive. Still, I fought them, wrestling the roller coaster of this forbidden love.

After several months of struggle, Brooke did what comes most naturally to people with a long history of trauma: she went into fight-or-flight mode. I wanted her to stay. I was still convinced we could face this head-on and work it through. Or, dreaming for the impossible, that maybe we might even actually have the potential of building a relationship together. Desperate for a way to make things okay, I even took the risk of speaking these dreams aloud to Brooke. But, overtaken by guilt and fear, Brooke made an impulsive decision to leave for the August kickoff of a different internship program in Michigan. She threw all of her stuff into her Toyota Corolla, and overnight, she was gone.

A flurry of emotions overtook me: devastation, confusion, hurt, overwhelming guilt, and a deep inner sadness—all feelings that I could share with no one because of the latent belief that our relationship was detestable in the eyes of God. We tried to navigate this bumpy road with occasional phone conversations, but got nowhere.

Despite it all, I was bound and determined to keep a promise I'd made earlier in the year to take her to visit her dad's grave for the five-year anniversary of his death. She had lost enough in her life, and I knew she needed this. We made a long weekend out of it and both agreed ahead of time to abstain from anything sexual while we were there. I was resolute in my determination to keep things platonic, or so I thought.

Lack of romantic experience kept me from realizing that distance does indeed make the heart grow fonder. Seeing each other after nearly two months apart provoked a wave of passion that overtook us when we reunited at the airport. I wrestled, trying to suppress those feelings and stay true to our agreement. But the tension was obvious.

After months of internal wrestling against something that felt so right, in the room we shared at the bed-and-breakfast that night, I decided to stop fighting so hard against this desire to love that ran so deep. I knew that sooner or later, I was going to have to face my fear of this fatal attraction. Putting my mind on pause, I decided that—just once—I would put perfection aside and allow my heart to lead the way.

When the sun went down and bedtime came, I lowered my emotional guard as we both crawled into a shared queen bed. But before turning off the light, I looked at the purity ring on my finger, a symbol that had carried me for the past ten years. I was aware of what it represented but was also aware that something deeper was going on inside me than the routine romantic attraction I'd watched some of my friends experience. I needed to figure out what it was. Knowing full well what I was doing and what it meant, I slipped the ring off my finger. Setting it on the nightstand beside me, with my heart open and my body vulnerable, I took one last glance at it and then reached over, and switched off the light.

Chapter 8

THE SACRED WEAPON

Several years after coming out, I bought my first home. In preparation to move in, I went through and sorted all the memorabilia I'd accumulated over the years. The day I went through my hope chest was an emotional one. It was the same hope chest my parents had given me at my thirteenth birthday party—the ceremony at which I'd committed myself to sexual purity until marriage and was given the ring by my dad to wear until I met my future husband. On the cedar floor of the chest, I found my purity ring. Dark and tarnished, it immediately took me back to that night at the bed-and-breakfast with Brooke, when I took it off forever.

I intentionally gave Brooke my virginity that night. It was a decision I made, assuming both its risks and consequences. In some ways, I regretted it deeply. The shame and remorse that followed me afterward felt completely overpowering at times. But in other ways, I didn't regret it at all. I loved Brooke. I wanted to know her without limitations. And honestly, I'm not sure what else would have catapulted me into my journey of discovering my sexuality, had I not taken that risk. Regardless of regret, that night we spent together changed the trajectory of my life.

It's a night that would have been steeped in beauty had it not been tainted by shame and the belief that what we were doing was sinful. I tried hard to silence the condemning voices in my head as we rustled beneath the sheets that night. I wanted to be in the moment, because the truth is, if I could put shame aside, the moment was beautiful. It was perfect. It was love at its most passionate. So I did my best to let go and give her my all. It was freeing to finally give in without feeling that need to resist. I felt relieved in a way. We had fought against this pull of forbidden love for months, and finally, that night, I made the conscious decision to stop fighting.

Following our weekend together, Brooke returned to her internship program in Michigan. We had several follow-up conversations about what that weekend meant for her now that she was back in the program. Should she be honest and tell somebody? Or should she keep it a secret? Having gone through my fair share of church internships and programs, I knew that keeping secrets from your leaders was never good. But I also knew that telling them the truth would get her kicked out of the program. There was rarely wiggle room for forgiveness in those types of internships. Like a Christian militia, you go in knowing what's expected of you, and if you don't measure up, you're out.

I knew I couldn't tell her what to do. So instead, I encouraged her to think about what she wanted in the long run. It wasn't long before guilt got the best of her and convinced her to confess. She was instantly kicked out of the program and sent home. Sexual behavior of any kind while in the program was prohibited, but same-sex behavior was even more forbidden. Soon thereafter, she showed up on my doorstep, asking for a second chance at living with me. I reluctantly said yes.

Having had my heart broken the first time Brooke left, I was hesitant to let her live with me again. Part of me wanted to make things right and just go back to being her friend, roommate, and mentor, like when we had first met. I thought maybe if we could do that, then it would be as if none of the sexual stuff had ever happened. But I knew backpedaling from sleeping together would be a hard line to draw. I wanted to believe that we were strong enough. Looking back, I realize I was only kidding myself. We loved each other, and being roommates or friends wasn't going to happen.

I did wonder if we could actually be in a romantic relationship with one another. I was discouraged by the marriages I saw around me during that time. Even with organizations like FOTF emphasizing the importance of marriage and family, it seemed as though almost everyone I knew, regardless of age or length of relationship, had gone through an affair or divorce. With divorce statistics being just as high among Christians as they are among the population at large, I was not optimistic about a lasting marriage to the someday husband that I had dreamed of all my life. So, if I already knew I loved Brooke, wasn't it better to be with someone I loved, even though she was a woman, instead of hoping for a fantasy that might only break my heart, if it ever even came true? But that was an unrealistic pipe dream, and Brooke and I both knew it. According to the tenets of our Christian faith and upbringings, being in a real romantic relationship with each other just wasn't an option.

It took only three short weeks after she returned to live with me before guilt ate away at Brooke enough for her to flee a second time. But this time, she decided to pay a visit to my parents before leaving town, and out our relationship to them. Then, once again, she disappeared.

My parents showed up on my doorstep at 6 a.m. the next day, texting me just before they arrived to say they were on their way over. We lived less than five minutes from one another, so there was essentially no time to prepare myself. I knew this wasn't good. Deep down, I desperately hoped that they would arrive bearing hugs of parental love and understanding. I needed a good cry after all this. I was only twenty-four, after all, and I longed for someone to tell me that everything was going to be okay. But instead, they stormed in, barely making eye contact with me, and sat down, ready to interrogate.

"Has this happened before? How long has this been going on, Amber? How old is she?" they fired, insinuating that this had gone on the whole time Brooke and I knew each other, or worse, that she was underage and I could be accused of having sex with a minor. It hurt me to the core. Nitpicking through my past, they searched for a point on which to pin the blame. Their long list of questions implied that I'd been hiding this dirty secret from them for years and manipulating them to believe that my hair-pulling, anxiety, and need for counseling all stemmed from other places, when I knew *this* was really the root of my struggles.

I assured them that was not the case and that this situation was just as much a shock to me when it happened as it was to them when they found out. But I could see in their eyes that they struggled to believe me. I was humiliated and ashamed. In reality, a lot of my earlier struggles in life likely did have to do with my sexuality, but I was so swaddled in a Christian cocoon that I had no way of even knowing that. FOTF made it clear that traditional marriage (between one man and one woman) was the only marriage that the Bible supports. Divorce was wrong, living with (or having sex with) someone outside of marriage was wrong—and queer relationships were *really* wrong. James Dobson taught that gay people were a threat to traditional marriage and made statements like, "If traditional marriage is not the law of the land, the institution of the family will cease to exist." Clearly, my actions were unacceptable, especially for a daughter with the perfect FOTF upbringing—and a daughter of an FOTF employee no less!

My parents were ashamed, disheartened, and embarrassed by me. I had let them down and failed to uphold the reputation of our family. It was obvious that they were deeply concerned for how this would affect our standing in the evangelical world where we were so highly admired.

I blinked back tears, trying to hide my own disappointment and pain. Even though I had begun questioning some of the beliefs taught to me growing up, I wasn't ready to admit that yet. Looking through the lens of my upbringing, punishment was what I deserved. Yet, what I really wanted was empathy and understanding. I tried to buck up and accept their rebuke, but I was broken and afraid.

My parents ended the meeting by saying, "Don't *ever* tell anyone about this, Amber, because if you do, it will ruin your reputation forever." Then, without even a hug goodbye, they walked out the door.

First I was scared, then I was interrogated, and now I was alone.

I realize now that it wasn't really *my* reputation my parents were worried about, but their own. They were concerned that my dad's long-term, high-powered position at FOTF could be in jeopardy if it got out. They were worried about what people would think. They were afraid of how they would be viewed as parents. They were scared it would tarnish their character and everything they'd worked to build their name on. But in the heat of the moment that day, it didn't matter whether it was my reputation on the line or theirs. We were still a family unit. The actions of one affected all. This theme had been strongly emphasized in our family, so a part of me felt obligated to keep this secret out of duty to my family name. More than once while I was growing up, my mom told me, "Amber, what you do reflects on us." What other people thought mattered a great deal.

This was the beginning of the unraveling. But it didn't have to be. The unraveling only began because our belief system came with black-and-white boundaries that denied us the opportunity to question what we believe, do our own research, trust our gut, or think outside the small box designed for our faith. Without permission to incorporate these critical components and without freedom to think for one's self, we are left with only two options: continue to live within the confines of our boxed-in beliefs, or allow our belief system to begin unraveling.

The recently released documentary *1946: The Mistranslation That Shifted Culture* reveals that the first time the word "homosexual" appeared in the Bible was in 1946 when the Revised Standard Version (RSV) translation team erroneously combined two independent words as "homosexual."[1] Because evangelicals believe in the literal interpretation of the Bible, with little thought for the involvement of human translators, we were taught that the word "homosexual" has been in the Bible for as long as the Bible has been around. But that simply is not true. At the writing of this book, the word "homosexual" has only been in the Bible for seventy-seven years. That is within many of our parents' or grandparents' lifetimes.

David Fearon, who was a twenty-one-year-old seminary student at the time, wrote to the translation team that he believed that they had "a serious weakness in translation" and that he feared "misinformed and misguided people may use the RSV translation of 1 Cor. 6:9–10 as a sacred weapon."[2] But the translation using the word "homosexual" had already been published, which then funneled through to the other mainline translations. Not only that, but the RSV was the translation of the Bible that was given out at Billy Graham crusades, expediting the widespread damage and catapulting this "sacred weapon" into the hands of religious leaders all over the nation. Though the translation was corrected a number of years later, the damage had already been done.

Today there are forty-five thousand evangelical churches in the United States. They still believe that being LGBTQ+ is a sin and continue to propagate messages of hate, homophobia, and transphobia. Their influence is largely responsible for the number of hate crimes we see against queer people, the number of LGBTQ+ people who have been shunned by their families, and the number of suicides that have taken place as a result. Compared to their peers, LGBTQ youth are more than four times as likely to attempt suicide. Only 37 percent of LGBTQ youth say their home is affirming, and those who face high levels of parental rejection are eight times more likely to attempt suicide and six times more likely to experience high levels of depression.[3] This powerful empire, these Bible-wielding gatekeepers, and these grim statistics were what I was up against at 6 a.m. that day as my parents interrogated me before the sun rose.

I was overwhelmed with confusion and fright. And so, like the good, people-pleasing, rule-following daughter I had always been, I did what they said and didn't tell a soul. I used my skill of compartmentalizing to stuff my emotions deep down inside, where they could hide forever, and I never spoke about it to anyone.

I also made a vow to myself that day that I couldn't cry. I wasn't allowed to cry. I didn't *deserve* to cry. The pain this time was *my* fault. I had screwed up. Therefore, I didn't have permission to grieve. I deserved what I got, and for the next ten excruciating months, that inner vow kept me silenced.

So many feelings and questions bombarded me in the months following that conversation with my parents. Having a relationship with a girl was, in the eyes of my family, the ultimate form of failure. Not only had I broken the vow I made at thirteen to stay sexually pure until my wedding day, but I did it with someone of the same gender—something I'd been taught that the Bible vehemently forbids. And to top it off, it wasn't just any girl; this was a Christian girl for whom I was supposed to be a role model. The shame I felt polluted how I thought about myself for months.

My virginity was something I had always saved for my husband. Now that I had given that away, I was convinced that no godly, Christian man was ever going to want me. And even if I were able to find a man who was gracious enough to overlook it, I didn't even know what that would look like. Would I still get to wear white on my wedding day? Would I feel special like I'd always dreamed? Or would I walk down the aisle feeling dirty and tainted—stained by my past, knowing everyone else would see me that way too, if they only knew?

And what would I say to that someday husband? "Here's my purity ring. I'm sorry. I tried"? My entire worth had been wrapped up in my sexual purity. Now that was a gift I no longer had to give.

Of course, for girls like me, the Christian cliché was, "You can become a recycled virgin." I remember thinking,

"Recycled, my ass. Recycled meaning previously used, smashed down, and put back together from garbage."

That's how I felt: like used garbage. The purity ring had been a symbol of my desires and beliefs all my life. Now it was in the bottom of my purse, the tarnished silver serving as a constant reminder of how tarnished I felt inside. I knew I could never wear it again—I didn't deserve to. Yet I couldn't bring myself to throw it away either.

I'm sure my parents noticed that I wasn't wearing it anymore, but they never said anything. It was further proof that I could never be the perfect daughter they longed for. Our family was flawed because of me. I was the black sheep.

*Without being able to talk to anyone about my pain, it didn't take long before I turned back to the very thing I'd sworn never to do again: cutting. After almost five years clean, I relapsed, and hard. I began cutting not only on my thighs, but on my forearms as well. I graduated from shaving razors to a utility knife, each time cutting a little more than the last, until a sense of release finally washed over me. As if that weren't enough, I also took up rubber bands as a new form of self-injury. Sliding the thick band around my forearm, I'd pull it back and repeatedly snap it as hard as I could. Counting numbly to well over a hundred, I wouldn't stop snapping until my arm was covered in black-and-blue bruises.

*At times, it was a form of punishing myself, like penance for all the ways I'd screwed up with Brooke—all the ways I'd failed God, my family, my dreams, myself. Other

---

*Trigger warning: Please keep yourself safe and skip these two paragraphs if you feel that reading about self-injury may trigger you.

times, it was the only way I knew to feel or express my pain—
a visible sign of my inward turmoil. I delayed self-harm for
as long as I could, trying to save it as a last resort. But there
were days when self-harm was all I thought about, even as
I fought to keep myself from doing it. Sometimes I took a
pen or marker and wrote my emotions on my arm instead,
as a way to express my feelings without doing actual harm.
But in the end, the knife or rubber band almost always won
out, because the physical pain on my body was still easier to
bear than the emotional pain in my soul. Often the bruises
and scars from cutting would last for weeks, even months.
Hiding them from others by wearing hoodies and pants, I
found an odd sense of comfort when seeing them myself
at home. It was proof that my pain was real. If no one else
would validate my pain, then I would validate it myself. But
just like the secret my parents told me to hide forever, I hid
my scars as well. They affirmed my buried pain and were
the only evidence of what went on inside me.

The fact that I relapsed was devastating. On top of all
my other failures, it felt like the ultimate defeat. It was as if
this one mistake with Brooke negated all that God called me
to and permanently disqualified me from any future ministry. I was insufficient, dispensable, and quite sure God
would never use me again. I had failed in every way possible: I'd slept with the girl I was supposed to help, I'd broken
my vow of purity, I'd committed an unforgivable sin, *and*
I'd relapsed into cutting. I felt like the epitome of failure.

Life was looking pretty bleak. At that point, I still
hoped to marry a man. The fact that my first love and first
sexual experience were with a woman didn't convince me I
was gay just yet. Instead, I did the same thing as my parents:
chalked it all up to a big mistake that never should have
happened, stuffed it down deep, and tried to figure out how

to move forward from there. It wasn't enough yet to shatter my belief system, but it definitely pulled at a thread—a thread that, in time, led me on a journey of discovering who I truly am. But at that point I knew no other way, and I was still holding onto my beliefs of what I'd been taught was right. And I was held captive by a secret that, at least for the time being, I told to no one.

As far as I knew, the only people who were aware of what had happened between me and Brooke (other than the two of us) were Pastor Sharon, a few people that Brooke trusted, and my parents. The circle that held our secret was still quite small. But paranoia crept in. I was sure if any of my peers knew, they would never want to spend time with me again. I was teaching piano lessons at the time, and I was certain that if the parents of my students knew, they would never leave their child alone with me again. I was convinced if people at church knew, they'd never let me serve in ministry again.

Even though none of these other people actually knew, I knew. And I couldn't stop wondering how everyone would treat me if they found out the truth of who I was and what I'd done. This is the mental torment that comes as a by-product of being conditioned to believe that God hates you.

During those ten months of suffering in silence, Brooke called me occasionally, even though her pastor told her not to. Sometimes she would break all contact, only to reach out to me again out of a desire for love and connection. It was an exhausting, terrible cycle that became more depleting with each round.

Eventually, I had to cut ties with Brooke for good. I still longed to be a source of support to her as promised. I wanted to be a listening ear in times of need. But I could no longer offer her that. I felt the way I imagine Lena may have felt when she walked out on me. Even though the situations were very different, my experience with Brooke helped me understand Lena a little more. But I didn't like feeling that way. I wanted to be better than Lena, tougher than Lena, stronger than Lena. But I had to come to terms with the fact that I couldn't save or change Brooke. I had to set her free to live her own life, so that I could be free myself.

Freedom. That's what I longed for. I felt shackled by pain and failure and disappointment and silence for so long. I wanted to be free. My heart was suffocating and gasping for air. Now, with my relationship with Brooke finally behind me, after ten months of denying myself the basic human right of tears, I finally broke down and cried. I couldn't bear the weight of it any longer.

Curled up on the floor in the back corner of church one night, I cried and cried and cried. For some time, I'd been afraid of releasing my pain. I wasn't sure I could handle the strong force of emotions that would come running out of a dam that had been so well built to protect my heart. Yet I was desperate to feel again—something, anything other than agony and disgrace. I was so ashamed: ashamed to approach my family, ashamed to approach God, ashamed to even look at myself. I longed to be free: free from guilt, free from shame, free from keeping secrets. Now that the nightmare with Brooke was finally over, I could start taking care of myself. The time had come to start my own journey of healing and freedom.

Chapter 9

UNDOING THE DAMAGE OF CONVERSION THERAPY

In 2021, the documentary *Pray Away* released on Netflix, detailing the history and harms of conversion therapy. It chronicles the rise and fall of Exodus International, whose primary mission was to make people who were "struggling with homosexuality" straight. During its height, Exodus reportedly had more than four hundred local groups in seventeen countries.[1] But after thirty-plus years of "ministry," Exodus closed its doors in 2013, admitting that its attempts at changing people didn't work and, in fact, caused a great deal of harm. Even after the closing of Exodus, conversion therapy continued and is still very much alive in America. In fact, conversion therapy is still legal for minors in thirty states. The twenty states that do have laws banning conversion therapy only go so far as to restrict licensed mental health practitioners from using this harmful approach on minors.[2] The ban does not restrict the practice among religious providers, which is where the majority of conversion therapy takes place.

In the film's opening, *Pray Away* describes conversion therapy as "the attempt to change a person's sexual orientation or gender identity by a religious leader, licensed counselor, or in peer support groups."[3] However, I would take that definition a step further. I would argue that conversion therapy doesn't just exist behind the closed doors of programs like Exodus and Living Hope. Rather, conversion therapy exists in people's homes, around dinner tables, and in pulpits. I never attended a formal conversion therapy program, yet I definitely did not escape the harm of these toxic teachings.

Conversion therapy isn't just a program; it's a system of belief—a theology professing that being gay is so utterly abhorrent and sinful in the eyes of God that one must suppress who they are, convert (change or fix) their sexual orientation and/or gender identity, and become straight/cis in order to become acceptable in the eyes of God, and therefore acceptable in the eyes of their fellow Christian family, friends, and peers. Through pressure toward this unattainable goal, LGBTQ+ people who are subjected to conversion therapy (which in some instances goes as far as including shock therapy) are being programmed to hate themselves and brainwashed into believing they must change in order to be loved by God and escape eternal torment in hell. I experienced all of this.

The documentary features Julie Rodgers, Yvette Cantu, and John Paulk, all of whom Exodus put on a pedestal as spokespeople for the movement—success stories proving it was possible to change. Grappling with an incredible amount of shame and the desire to be accepted by their community, they did what was expected of them. They followed the rules, they shared their stories of supposed conversion, and they advocated for others to do the same. The pressure put on them to conform worked in Exodus's favor, providing "evidence" that not only were straight people telling gay people they needed to change, but people who previously identified as gay (or "same-sex attracted"—the preferred term in lieu of claiming an ingrained orientation) were telling them it was possible.

However, the former leaders featured in this film admit that ex-gay therapy didn't truly help anyone become "ex-gay." It was merely successful at behavior modification (shame and shunning have a way of doing that), but it was not at all successful in actually "fixing" or "converting" people from gay to straight. The feelings, desires, and attractions remained—the people simply continued to ignore, suppress, and deny them.

This theory of being "fixed" also does not account for people who are bisexual, like Yvette Cantu. At the time she claimed she was a lesbian who became straight, but now she acknowledges that she is attracted to both sexes, although she has been married to a man for many years.

The effects of this movement have done extreme harm to the LGBTQ+ community, especially those from conservative Christian or evangelical backgrounds. The film states that more than seven hundred thousand people have gone through some form of conversion therapy in the United States alone. While that tally may reflect the number of actual participants in reparative therapy programs, I believe the conversion therapy movement's reach and impact on LGBTQ+ people, including people like me, is far greater than that, likely in the millions.

There are many survivors, but not all survived. A national survey found that LGBTQ youth who experienced conversion therapy were more than twice as likely to attempt suicide.[4] This practice is psychologically damaging and induces such great amounts of self-hatred and shame that intensive work and therapy are required to undo the mental programming. For some, undoing that programming is almost impossible.

With more than twenty years of study on the topic of shame, researcher and storyteller Dr. Brené Brown defines shame as "the intensely painful feeling or experience of believing we are flawed and therefore unworthy of acceptance and belonging."[5]

With that definition in mind, I began to realize that shame had been the root cause of almost every negative thing I had struggled with in my life.

I felt shame when I thought about my hair-pulling disorder and how self-conscious it made me feel about my appearance.

I felt shame when thinking about being depressed or having anxiety and needing to go to therapy.

I felt shame about the fact that I self-harmed. It was proof that I couldn't hold everything together. Even more shame washed over me when I relapsed after five years clean.

I felt shame for embarrassing my family with what they considered to be sinful behavior with Brooke. Losing my purity, especially in *that* way, definitely did not uphold the family name in the way they expected of me.

I've become increasingly aware that shame played a much bigger role in my pre-coming-out life than I ever would have liked. In a way, coming out was an intentional decision to recognize shame for the toxic, suffocating, manipulative tool that it is, and to walk away from it. Shame does not have a role in my life now like it did prior to my coming out. So much of that shame stemmed from the church. Judgment from people acting in the name of God planted my seeds of self-hatred and shame.

I remember the first time I saw Brooke laid out on the bed fully naked. She was so beautiful, it took my breath away. I know the first time she saw me unclothed, she thought the same. We were so in love. But because our families and our churches told us it was wrong to love another woman, our love was contaminated by shame. What could our relationship have looked like if neither of us had been taught that queer relationships were wrong and sinful? It wouldn't have been a lasting relationship—we both carried too much baggage at that time—but we would have been free of all the needless turmoil and agony brought on by shame.

After cutting ties with Brooke, I began an inner pilgrimage to find freedom from shame. I was sick of cheap imitations of the voice of God handed to me by others and needed to rekindle my own relationship with the Creator of my heart.

What I didn't realize at the time was that while those ten months of holding everything inside may have protected my reputation from the judgment of others, they also isolated me from love—love from others and also love from God. Steeped in shame, I didn't believe I deserved to approach God. I felt frail, alone, and vulnerable. My raw humanity felt at odds with a God whose love seemed—as I understood it based on my upbringing—to be conditional. My church and family proclaimed the unconditional love of God with their lips, but then taught me with their actions that God only loves you if you're good and follow the rules with complete devotion. If you make a mistake (especially a mistake as bad as mine), then you are bad, and God is mad at you and abhors your behavior. It may not have been explicitly stated that way, but the implication was clear.

It was clear from the pulpit when youth pastors emphasized the importance of spending at least one hour in prayer and Bible study every day. Anything less was subpar. It was clear from the FOTF teachings that you fight against the temptations of your body in order to please God.

Failure to do this was weakness and lack of faith and perseverance. It was clear in the faces of my parents when they heard about my relationship with Brooke. They were angry with me. God was angry with me. I hadn't measured up.

This wasn't the God I knew in my teen years. The moments we spent together were so sweet and precious. Now I felt split between what I knew of God personally and what prominent Christian leaders were teaching me about God. That confusion launched me into my own journey of exploration. I began to wrestle with God and the questions that bombarded my heart.

Up until that point in my life, I largely thought the way I was conditioned to think. As intended, my parents were living out the eugenic goal of the evangelical system that encouraged encasing your children in order to generate more of the desired type of "fit" humans. They embraced and implemented the FOTF ideal of creating a completely Christian-packaged environment. Homeschooling in place of public school, church programs instead of school clubs, vacation Bible school instead of sports camp, Awana in lieu of Girl Scouts and Boy Scouts, mission trips in exchange for humanitarian projects—all to protect us from the "outside world" and mold us into advocates and defenders of the movement who would replicate the system for the generation to come. Being swaddled in an alternative reality did nothing to prepare me for the real world. But that was intentional, because the goal is to keep one ensconced in this subculture as an adult and convince them to perpetuate the system by getting married, serving in ministry, and raising a family of their own on these same beliefs.

I wasn't given an opportunity to think critically for myself. I was told what to think and how I should feel in almost every situation, like a Christian clone. As a result,

I had no tools to be my own person and find my own way in the world. I was told to defend what I believed, but was never given a fair chance to decide if they were beliefs that I wanted to defend. Without exposure to diversity (people of color, people with disabilities, people of different sexual orientations, gender identities, and belief systems) I wasn't able to appreciate and respect all the different shapes and forms that God comes in. That knowledge would have helped me appreciate the world at large at a much younger age and also be more in tune with myself.

Instead, I was taught to love everyone, but with the condition that we love them in order to make them like us: faithful, committed Christians who love God and do what the Bible commands. If they weren't Christians, then the goal was to convince them to want to become one. If they were Christians, then the goal was to "be a blessing to them" just as my mom trained us to do. I did many great things in order to bless and serve others—I sang and performed all over the world, I went on mission trips, I reached out to people who were struggling—but looking back, I wish I had done more of it without strings attached. Yet that was all I knew to do. I had become a Christian cliché. But now, it was proving painful.

At the age of twenty-six, I finally started to break out of that mold. It was long overdue. Though it was intimidating at first, I finally began thinking for myself and developing my own worldview, instead of seeing through the lens of my parents' worldview. It was the first time I'd begun to wonder what the world looked like outside this evangelical box I lived in. However, having been conditioned not to trust myself or anything outside this box, I also doubted myself and the part of me that had already taken steps to follow my heart rather than the path prescribed for me. It's as if the evangelical system came with a built-in gaslighting function designed to convince me I was crazy for trying to escape. I asked myself questions like these:

> Am I deceived to believe that I did the right thing in taking Brooke into my home?
> Is what everyone said about Brooke and me true, and I'm the one believing the lie?
> Is my soul now damned to hell for what happened between us?
> Did I really even hear God in the first place?

I was so sure when I first met Brooke that I was supposed to let her live with me. But now, several months after she left, I doubted. I wondered where I went wrong along the way.

Then I started asking other questions:

> Why have I never had a boyfriend?
> Why have I never been asked out on a date?
> Why have I never been kissed?
> Why do I not even think about boys the way my friends do?
> Is there something wrong with me?

I decided two things were necessary: therapy and dating. I figured the answer to these confusing and heart-wrenching questions might lie in the fact that I had never been on a date with anyone . . . ever! And if the answers didn't lie in dating, then surely they would lie inside a therapist's office. I simultaneously enrolled myself in both dating and therapy.

Morgan was my new therapist, and she let me bring all parts of myself to the table: my faith, my family, my sexuality, my questions; there weren't any limitations when I came to her office. She even let me bring my Shih Tzu–Maltese puppy, Half Pint, because she knew it was helpful and calming for me. Morgan was the first person to give me permission to explore who I was. No one had done that for me before.

Each week I came with my heavy heart and we unpacked a little more. I told her my fear of going to hell. I explained to her the Christian belief that being gay put my soul in jeopardy. I opened up and told her that every time something went wrong in my life—a bad day, a flat tire, an unexpected death—I felt it was God's punishment for the feelings I harbored inside. I desperately wanted to get rid of them. I wanted to be normal. But no matter how hard I tried, the feelings wouldn't go away. My anxiety rose higher and higher as I feared what would happen to me if I got in a fatal car crash or went to bed one night and simply didn't wake up. Would my soul be damned to an eternity in hell because I hadn't been able to resolve or pray away my gay feelings? Would I be separated from my family and friends and all those I love forever because there was a part of me that I didn't ask for, yet couldn't get rid of? I just wanted to be like everyone else. I wanted to belong. I felt so isolated and alone in my fear.

Week after week, Morgan helped me process my fears as we sorted through my emotions around Brooke, around my parents, around my faith, around life after death, and around my sexuality. She gave me permission to be free from the pressure of labeling myself as gay or straight.

One day I walked into counseling to find Morgan sitting there with a basket of rocks and a marker. She explained that on each rock, she wanted me to write a feeling, a struggle, or the name of a person. Then, when I was through, I would tell her what each represented and why I'd chosen it. It was meant to be a tangible representation of my inward struggles.

I sat for a moment, pondering the names of my rocks. Then, getting up from the couch and sitting on the floor, I dumped them all in a pile. On the first rock, I wrote **Me,** and placed it in the middle of the floor. I wrote **Lesbian???/Scared of Hell** on another rock and set it down. On the next I wrote **Shame,** and then set it aside. After getting started, I was on a roll and continued with rocks labeled **Mom/Dad, Daniel,** and **God.** Then I went on labeling others with words like **PTSD, Stuffed Emotions, Hair-Pulling, Self-Harm,** and on it went. I came up with so many labels that I ran out of rocks and Morgan had to go to the parking lot to collect more.

I don't think this was part of the assignment, but I then started arranging the rocks on the carpet like a puzzle. With the rock representing me at the center, I placed each of the other rocks around it in relation to where I felt they were in my life. Morgan sat patiently as I worked in silence for a good ten minutes. When I finished, I sat back and looked at her. She nodded and said, "Okay. Tell me about your rocks."

I explained to her this newfound map of my life, telling her where I placed everything and why. I placed the **PTSD** rock together with the ones labeled **Stuffed Emotions** and **Hair-Pulling** because they seemed to come hand in hand, though they didn't surface every day. They were stationed in the top left corner of my life picture. I placed the **Mom/Dad** rock as well as the one for my brother **Daniel** far away in the top right corner with another one labeled **Outcast** directly on top of them, indicating with the distance that I was having to pull away from them more and more because outcast is how being around them made me feel. I placed **God** fairly close to **Me** but just a little apart because I wasn't sure how all these struggles made me feel about God, or how God felt about me. Afraid that the possibility of being gay would damn my soul to hell, I was confused about the love versus the judgment of God.

The more I explained this visual representation of my emotions to my counselor, the more therapeutic it became. It helped me make sense of my life and gave me the opportunity to look at it in an organized fashion, manipulating the location of the different pieces based on how I felt about each. It gave me a sense of control when so many things in my life felt so out of control.

It also gave me the chance to identify my emotions. My upbringing denied me the chance to explore feelings the way I should have. I often struggled to express myself and had difficulty labeling what I was feeling when emotions other than happiness surfaced. They felt like a jumbled mess inside. At least with my rocks, my feelings had a name. Labeling them helped me understand them, which in turn helped me better understand my life as a whole.

Envisioning my map of rocks helped me start to make sense of the war raging inside me. I felt divided. It was as if half of me belonged in one world and half of me belonged in another, and it seemed impossible that these two worlds would ever meld into one. I was facing an ultimatum between my faith in God and my sexuality. I was unable to deny my love for Jesus, but equally powerless to make my love and attraction toward women disappear. No matter how hard I prayed or how many good things I did or how hard I tried to like boys, this disjointed feeling wouldn't dissipate. It tore my heart in two. Fasting and praying, I begged God to take these feelings away from me, to heal me, to make me normal; I promised anything in return. I loved Jesus! I didn't want to go to hell! I didn't want to be separated from my family or lose my friends!

"Haven't I been through enough?" I'd shout at God. "Why this? Why *me*?"

The complexity of this war inside overwhelmed me—I can only describe it as torture. I reached a point where I realized that if I didn't face this and find a way to make peace with it, it was going to be the thing that killed me. I had endured years of feeling at odds within myself and I was now at the point where I knew I couldn't survive it much longer. Thoughts of suicide began to haunt me. I didn't know where or how. I just knew how isolated I felt in my struggle and how limited and bleak my options were. The scrutinizing eyes and whispers behind my back from friends and family told me I was unlovable. It taught me to be ashamed of who I was. I knew I had to find answers. If I wanted to survive, I had to fight for my life. I had to fight for me since no one else would. Part of sorting through those emotions came by working with my basket of rocks.

Morgan held on to my basket of rocks for me from week to week, and occasionally we pulled them out and reassessed how things were going. I moved the rocks closer or farther apart than in previous meetings based on how things in my life were progressing. Over time, if I settled a certain issue, that rock was thrown away. But likewise, as we went on, new rocks were added, such as **Coming Out, Fear of Rejection,** and **Desire for Girlfriend?** In all the counseling I've had over the years, this was the single most effective exercise I've ever done.

While working through things in therapy, I also worked on the second half of the puzzle and reluctantly went on some dates with men. Knowing this was the fairy tale I was supposed to want, I tried my best to go with an open mind and have a good time. But in reality, I never enjoyed it much. It's not that I'm repulsed by men (though some of them were quite repulsive); I just didn't feel anything—no connection, no spark, no butterflies. I enjoyed the attention but felt edgy, awkward, and uncomfortable around them, not excited.

There was one exception: Darius. If I ever had a chance at a successful straight relationship, Darius was it. We got to know one another and there was a connection . . . of sorts. I certainly enjoyed being with Darius more than any of the other guys I went out with. Haunted by the straight person's myth that "you just haven't met the right guy yet," or the skeptic's theory that "you just don't like guys because you've never been with one," I decided that if I was going to end up being gay, it wouldn't be for lack of trying to be straight. So I gave it my all.

One huge surprise for me as I began to date men was that my virginity (or, at least, the fact that I had never had sex with a man) wasn't valued by these men the way I expected it to be. Contrary to what I was taught, the men I met were actually intimidated by my lack of experience, including Darius. It caused me to feel embarrassed by my virginity, not proud. Another disservice given to me by purity culture, I was ill prepared for life outside my Christian bubble.

Ultimately, the pressure to fit into society's norms led me to have sex with Darius. I felt obligated to do it because of evangelicalism, in a weird sort of way. On one hand, sex outside of marriage was a sin highly frowned upon. On the other hand, if I was gay, I felt I owed it to my faith somehow to prove that I'd given being straight my best attempt.

Sleeping with Darius turned out to be eye-opening. This was the moment I'd waited for all my life. Though we certainly didn't "save sex for marriage" as evangelicalism taught, I still expected this moment to somehow launch me into sexual bliss as a reward for all the years I'd saved myself and waited. Maybe deep down, I did expect it to make me straight. But that's *not* what happened. Instead, I was disappointed. There was no inner excitement over having sex with a man for the first time. Instead, I felt cheated. I found myself thinking, *I've waited all my life . . . for this???* It was completely unsatisfying. I know that for most people (especially straight women) the first time isn't always pleasurable, but the emotional connection between Darius and me wasn't anything like the emotional connection I felt with Brooke. Being with Brooke was natural and easy and electric. Being with Darius was awkward and forced and uncomfortable. I left that night feeling deceived by Christians and the purity culture I'd been a part of.

In the days following, I found that I hardly gave that night with Darius a second thought. It felt meaningless to me. So I stepped outside the lines a little more and dated a few women. It was a risk that I spoke of to no one, yet felt I had to take. After several dates with one woman, we kissed. Then I realized something. I found myself obsessing way more over this girl I'd simply kissed than I thought about the entire sexual experience I'd shared with Darius.

That's when the lightbulb came on: there was a significant difference for me in the connection I felt with each sex. I'd known each of them about the same amount of time, but when I thought about my simple kiss with this girl, it made my head spin and sent butterflies to my stomach. When I thought about my time with Darius, I felt nothing. Deep inside I knew then that I was gay. I still wasn't ready to admit it, however, even to myself, because I still didn't know what being gay would mean for my relationship with God.

On my way out of the grocery store one afternoon, I stopped by Redbox to see the lineup of new movies. Scrolling through the titles on the screen, there was one I hadn't heard of before, *Prayers for Bobby*. A Lifetime film starring Sigourney Weaver, it caught my attention, and I clicked on the title for more information. Reading the film description, I saw two words I'd never seen put side by side: *gay* and *Christian*. My eyes widened. *You mean, this is a thing? I'm not the only one who feels like a social and religious outcast?* Eager to know more, I swiped my card to pay for the film and took it home.

In the privacy of my bedroom that night, I watched the true story of a boy named Bobby Griffith. He was the perfect son, the favorite child—until Bobby realized he was gay and came out to his family. This caused Bobby's mother, Mary, to turn to her conservative and fundamentalist beliefs in an attempt to rescue Bobby from what she felt was the unforgivable sin.

During the first half of the movie, so much of it paralleled my own life that it was painful. This was *my* life I was watching. The way Bobby confided only in his journals was just like me. The anxiety he confessed over going to hell was the same anxiety I felt. The fear over losing his family, his friends, and all he held dear was the very fear I was facing. The way his prayers never seemed to be enough to rid him of his gayness, the pressure he felt to conform to his family's desires, the way he was told he wasn't being healed because he didn't have enough faith and wasn't trying hard enough—all of this mirrored *my* very deep and painful experience. My eyes were glued to the screen.

*Once Bobby's mom realized that her efforts at saving Bobby weren't producing any change, she did the very thing Bobby feared most: she rejected him. The pain and exclusion Bobby felt quickly became too much for him to bear. Despair overtook him and darkness set in. Overcome by the war raging inside him and the pain of being ostracized, Bobby jumped from a highway overpass one night, taking his own life.

Now I was sobbing. I related to that crushing fear of being rejected by those you love the most. I feared that Bobby's fate would be my own. I knew the feeling of being at the end of your rope. I knew the isolation and intense loneliness of wrestling with the unspeakable. I knew the overwhelming seas of emotion.

After Bobby's death, Mary searched for a place to pin the blame. Eventually, out of desperation and struggle, she reached out to an affirming pastor in the gay community. Meeting with him, Mary was finally able to see the love of God for all the diversity it really holds. In the dim light of a chapel on a rainy night, Mary broke down in tears as she came to the realization that her own ignorance and lack of acceptance is what really killed her son.

I cried for Mary. I cried for Bobby. I cried for me. The story of the Griffith family foretold my story as I saw it unfolding in the months to come. It magnified my hidden fears and put them right before my eyes. I trembled inside at the thought that my life was about to unravel.

At this point, things in my life were still somewhat intact. I had cleaned up the outward pieces from the mess with Brooke and escaped with only my parents knowing

---

*Trigger warning: Please keep yourself safe and skip this paragraph if you feel that reading about suicide may trigger you.

about it. My parents and I still spent time together frequently, and the awkward moments between us around what had happened with Brooke were minimal. They were just as good at compartmentalizing as I was. Though they did start analyzing my friends a lot more closely, they didn't mention Brooke very often. Instead, they chose to see the whole situation as a big mistake. Like everything else, they wanted to just sweep it under the rug, forget about it, and move on with our Focus on the Family façade.

That was fine with me. I knew already from my parents' reaction when they heard about Brooke that involving them in my exploration of sexuality and faith wasn't an option. I did what I had to do to please them, while searching for truth on my own. They had already silenced me once. I wasn't going to let it happen again.

Watching *Prayers for Bobby* was the first time that I realized I was not alone in my struggle. Up until then, I thought that I was the only one in the world who was misfit enough to turn up gay in a "perfect" Christian family. But after seeing the movie, I saw that there was at least one other person like me. And if there was one, perhaps there were two, or three, or possibly more.

This epiphany led me to start researching who else might be out there like me. Previously, I thought that any organization or group of people that claimed to be both gay and Christian was a farce. It was impossible to be both. They were two opposing worlds that did *not* intersect. But now curiosity piqued my interest and I decided to risk looking outside my box a little further.

In order to do that, I needed to put some distance between me and the judgmental people in my life. I knew I couldn't hear the fresh voice of God if all that played in my head were negative tapes that God hated me. So I did my best to keep those voices at a distance. This included walking away from church for a time. With a clean slate, I began a new phase of my journey. Looking back, I realize there was real wisdom in this. Distancing myself from those negative voices and listening only to my own inner voice was indeed the very key to finding what set me free.

I was about to undertake what felt like an enormous endeavor: to search for others who, like me, were both gay and Christian, and also to finally look at what the Bible really said about queer relationships. I was terrified. I didn't want to "water down the gospel" just to make myself comfortable, nor did I want to miss a hidden truth of God just because I was comfortable in a box or listened to the wrong people. I was terrified to find out that God *did* approve of queer relationships and I was equally terrified to find out that God *did not* approve of them. I knew either way, my life was about to drastically change. Taking a deep breath, I sat down at my computer and opened my web browser, ready to start my quest for truth.

Chapter 10

BREAKING FREE FROM CHRISTIAN NATIONALISM

Over the last few years, we've started seeing more films about gay people coming out to their families. Movies like *Jenny's Wedding* and *Happiest Season* portray scenarios where women have to tell their family that they are gay in order to freely be with the person they love. While it's wonderful to have more queer representation in the media, these stories are also a reminder of the heartache that LGBTQ+ people carry simply for being who they are.

The fact that LGBTQ+ people still so often face discrimination and rejection from their families—which is largely based in the evangelical belief that being gay is a sin—is a prime example of Christian nationalism in America. What has been preached from the pulpit has taken root in the homes of American families—families that then fight with both their money and their vote to make sure that their Christian beliefs are the basis for how the country is legally run. Focused so intently on power, they completely lose sight of the fact that they are dehumanizing the very people they claim to love, stripping them of their most basic human rights. What started out as a mistranslation of biblical text has indeed become one of the biggest sacred weapons and culture wars of our time. Entire political platforms have been built around supporting and maintaining the institution of the White, straight, cisgender, Christian family.

The Moral Majority (founded by Jerry Falwell in 1979) built its platform on being "pro-family and pro-American" and fought against developments in civil rights, women's rights, and gay rights that (in their minds) threatened to undermine Christian marriage and family values. This effort proved successful almost immediately with the 1980 election of Ronald Reagan, who ran on a platform of creating a constitutional amendment that would ban abortion (despite having previously supported abortion rights himself). Though the Moral Majority was disbanded in 1989, it was credited for making a lasting impact on the political influence of the religious right.[1] Years later, we continue to see the influence of the religious right with the election of Donald Trump. Vowing to put power back in hands of Christian leaders and shift the culture war back in their favor is largely how Trump was elected in 2016. Trying to maintain that power at all costs in 2020—regardless of policies and procedures, or clear evidence that Trump had lost his run for a second term—is what led to the insurrection at the United States Capitol on January 6, 2021. So-called Christians were so desperate to maintain political power and control that they were willing to go to extreme lengths and illegal measures to achieve it.

A 2021 article about research at Washington University in St. Louis states that many Christians see the progress being made for LGBTQ+ people as an attack on Christianity. The three-and-a-half-year study found that "zero-sum beliefs" (the idea that one group's social gains require losses for another group) are driven by symbolic threats, not realistic ones. White, straight, cisgender Christians fear that greater social acceptance for queer people threatens their own social influence, mainly their ability to wield political power and shape the nation's policies to align with their own set of beliefs.[2]

Misguided information about the LGBTQ+ community and lack of education, exposure, or experience lead people to live in fear of what they don't know. Much of that misinformation is disseminated by people in power. An episode of James Dobson's *Family Talk* podcast featured a conversation with Franklin Graham in which Graham made extremely hateful comments regarding queer children.

> "We have allowed the enemy to come into our churches," Graham said. "I was talking to some Christians [who] invited these gay children to come into their home and to come to church, [because they wanted] to influence them. And I thought to myself, those parents aren't going to influence those kids; those kids are going to influence those parents' children. We have to understand who the enemy is and what he wants to do. He wants to devour our homes. He wants to devour this nation. We have to be so careful who we let our kids hang out with. We have to be so careful who we let into the churches. We have immoral people that get into our churches and it begins to affect the others in the church and it is dangerous. You cannot stay gay and call yourself a Christian."[3]

Dobson followed this comment with a horribly faulty and inaccurate definition of bisexuality: "You know what the 'B' [in LGBT] stands for? Bisexual. That's orgies! That's lots of sex with lots of people."

These erroneous comments shape the beliefs of evangelical Christians around the globe and provide a grossly misguided view of the LGBTQ+ community. They provoke hate and fear, and spread irreversibly damaging information about a group of minorities that struggle every day to simply exist in the world as they are without persecution.

After hearing these kinds of comments from the mouths of Dobson and Graham for years, I showed up to the Club Q memorial shortly following the massacre in November 2022 to find a group of people from Franklin Graham's "ministry team" on site, wanting to pray with and comfort people. It's not an understatement to say I about lost my shit. The very idea that they thought they had a right to be at this place of sacred grief was completely repulsive and made me absolutely sick to my stomach. I am deeply grateful for the affirming clergy in the area who began showing up in shifts as a counteraction and to provide a truly safe and loving presence for all who were coming to grieve.

Mel White, executive director of SoulForce, along with many others, tried to warn Dobson of his harmful teachings years ago, when they protested Dobson's campaign against gay marriage at FOTF in 2005. "We are here to say, Jim, we love you enough to stop you from doing the damage you are doing to families across the nation," White said.[4]

If Dobson had taken to heart the message Mel White and others were communicating instead of brushing it aside as warped theology, he could have stopped these misguided beliefs and faulty teachings from affecting his 220 million followers worldwide. If he had listened, lives could have been saved, rather than lost to suicide and murder. If he had listened, families could have been strengthened and restored, rather than torn apart—perhaps my family could have been one of them. But instead, FOTF continues to have a political agenda and Dobson's teachings continue to harm countless gay Christians and their families, driving many away from the church and from God.

Education and exposure make all the difference. Many people find that once they get to know a gay or transgender person, the myths of what they thought queer people to be are exposed as null and void, and they realize that LGBTQ+ people (like most people) just want to be themselves and be loved as they are. Proximity to the LGBTQ+ community changes perspectives. It's a lot easier to consider queer relationships dirty, disgusting, or even sinful when you don't know any queer people. It's a lot harder when that person or people group you've been mocking turns out to be your best friend, your brother, your cousin, or your aunt. A 2019 study from The Trevor Project also found that "LGBTQ youth who report having at least one accepting adult were 40% less likely to report a suicide attempt in the past year."[5] *One accepting adult.*

For me, that came in the form of finding my first affirming faith community. Sitting at my computer one morning, I decided I was ready to begin my quest for truth. I needed to know for myself how God really felt about LGBTQ+ people and queer relationships. Timidly, I typed "Gay Christian Churches in Colorado" into my web browser. I forced a deep breath, allowing space to feel both fear and hope, and hit Enter, telling the search engine to comb the web for results.

Because Colorado Springs is a conservative, military town and the headquarters for numerous Christian ministries, I wasn't surprised that I didn't find much when it came to gay-affirming churches in my immediate area. But I kept searching. I didn't want to be accused of simply finding a group of people who "justified my way of life." I was looking for something that still resembled the evangelical style and beliefs of my upbringing, but also allowed space for bigger views on love—if that even existed.

The only church on the list that looked like even a remote possibility was a small church about seventy-five miles north of where I lived. Curious and desperate for a lifeline—anything that might offer me some hope—I clicked the link. The first thing I saw on their home page was their ethos. Tears welled in my eyes as I read it and saw that people of all sexual orientations, gender identities, abilities, ethnicities, and relationship statuses were embraced by this community. *Could this be real? Did a place for people like me, who were attracted to the same gender but really loved God, actually exist?* I decided to email the pastor and find out. Unsure whether I was writing out of hope or sheer desperation (or perhaps both), I poured out my broken heart to this pastor I had never met. I told him about Brooke, I told him about my family, I told him about my shame, I told him how bleak life was feeling, and I asked for help. Then, with trepidation, I took the risk of hitting Send.

I didn't have to wait long for a reply. Hardly three hours went by before I received a very long, heartfelt response from the founding pastor himself. I was shocked, after spending more than a decade at a church that had fourteen thousand members, where you were lucky if you ever heard from a secretary, let alone a pastor. It was humbling to read words of kindness from a man who, although he was straight, empathized with my struggle. With the compassion of a father, he expressed deep love for and acceptance of me. He spoke the words I was longing to hear but struggled to believe: God loves me exactly the way that I am and I don't have to change anything to be accepted by God. He extended an invitation to visit the church and said if I was interested, he would contact a couple of girls to show me around and take me to lunch after the service. It seemed too good to be true. Knowing the critical place I was in, I quickly replied and said yes.

Driving north that following Sunday, my heart raced at highway speed as my hands gripped the steering wheel tighter and tighter. I didn't know what to expect. I was afraid to get my hopes up only to be disappointed. But I needed this to be the answer I'd been searching for. Feeling unwelcome at church ever since the last time I trusted a pastor with my secret, it was vital to my soul that this experience be different. My very life was hanging in the balance.

I nervously parked in a small parking lot on the corner across the street and took a moment to breathe. The pastor had given me the contact information of two girls to meet up with. *Were they friends? Were they a couple?* I had no idea. Other than one of the girls I dated for a short time after Darius, I'd never met another openly gay person. This was new territory for me.

Part of me wondered how I would measure up against what I saw. Because I lacked exposure, I didn't know if it was even possible for a feminine-leaning girl like me to be gay. Was short hair or masculine clothes a qualifier? I had no idea. The answers to so many of my questions lay just inside those church doors on the other side of the parking lot.

The two girls, who of course were a couple, were waiting for me when I arrived. They looked extremely normal. In fact, as I looked around, I noticed that everyone inside looked normal. Women of all hair lengths and styles mingled—some in skirts or dresses, others in jeans and T-shirts. The men looked equally ordinary. Suit jackets, polo shirts, and jeans were mixed with clean-cut and scruffy hairstyles.

Having been repeatedly warned about the "gay agenda" and the liberals' attempt to overtake the nation and undermine traditional family values, this was not what

I expected. There were no rainbow flags or drag queens; there weren't any people making out in the lobby or protesters at the door with "God Hates Fags" signs. What I saw was not what I was taught to expect at a gathering that welcomed gay people. Now, I've since been to churches that do have drag queens and let me just tell you, drag queen church is some of the best church there is. But baby gay me wasn't quite ready for that just yet. On my first Sunday in this new church, these casual, normal-looking people who were gathering together, hugging and greeting one another as you would expect to see at any ordinary church, was just what I needed. I took mental notes on everything and adjusted my expectations accordingly as I stood in the lobby. I immediately experienced an overwhelming sense of authenticity, acceptance, and love. Perfect strangers warmly embraced me and welcomed me as though they'd known me all their lives. They seemed genuinely happy to meet me and have me there.

One tall, husky man heard it was my first time and that my dad worked at FOTF. He didn't even speak a word. He just moved in and gave me a big bear hug, as if to say, "Oh, honey, I can only imagine how much you must be going through." I almost broke down in tears right there.

As the service started, I took my seat and began to absorb the experience. After several songs, the founding pastor took the stage. The first words out of his mouth were those of the ethos I saw online. Hearing these words said aloud in this space made me feel safe in a church for the first time in almost five years. My heart began to melt, hanging on his every word.

". . . in imitation of the ridiculous love that almighty God has for each of us and all of us, we choose to live and love without labels. Amen?"

"Amen!" the congregation answered.

Without labels. I thought about that phrase for a moment, trying to wrap my mind around what that meant. I'd felt tied to labels for as long as I could remember. Was this man, this *pastor,* really releasing me from the weight of appearances I'd felt pressured to uphold my entire life? I'd always felt the need for labels. These descriptors explained to others who I was. I was a *Christian,* I was *homeschooled,* I was the *daughter of a high-powered Focus on the Family employee,* I was *Daniel's sister,* I was the *Green Gable Girls leader's daughter,* I was a *musician.* I was supposed to be *happy, blessed, a role model* for others. Labels defined me. Labels of shame, labels of perfection, labels of destruction. Some labels I still wrestled with. Was I gay or straight? Was I still a Christian, or did this new label come in exchange of the old one? Could I be both gay *and* Christian? So much depended on labels, on appearances, on acceptance. Was there really such a place where I could come and be free of all of these defining words that stuck to me and bogged me down?

As I listened to the pastor speak these words of acceptance and life, my feelings of isolation softened a bit. I could feel the Spirit whispering to me that this was the safe place I'd been searching for. I had finally found other people like me and a sanctuary for my heart to rest.

As I've continued to evolve over the last ten years, my views on this phrase, "living and loving without labels," have changed. Reading it now, it feels like the equivalent of the phrase "I don't see color." Just as to see a Black person is to see their color and all that has been experienced by their race and embodied in their skin tone, the same is true of LGBTQ+ people. To see us is to see our queerness: the beautiful diversity we bring to the world, the struggles we face, and the marginalizations we encounter. You can't claim to love or see us without our LGBTQ+ label. To do so is to erase our very existence. We need to be seen, valued, and celebrated for all of who we are. I don't fault this church for the ethos they had at the time—they were actually on the cutting edge of the inclusion movement and leading other evangelical-style churches to become affirming. Their words were also deeply healing to me in a season when I deeply needed healing.

Gathering in a place where people could bring all of who they were was revolutionary for me. These people weren't afraid to question or doubt or explore their beliefs. They pushed past the boundaries that evangelical Christians tended to live within. They didn't feel threatened by new ideas or different interpretations of the Bible, the way so many other Christians I'd met seemed to be. It was a beautiful balance, and a freeing one. It was authentic, it was real, and my heart finally felt at home.

That day, January 8, 2012, was a turning point for me. I went home and wrote in my journal for the first time in three years, because it was the first time that I'd felt hope in three years.

I've passed the point of no return. I can feel it. Today I saw that it was possible to love God and a person of the same sex. I don't know what the future holds, but I know this new church has to be a part of it.

Chapter 11

ACCEPTANCE AND FREEDOM

I drove to my new church every Sunday that I could manage in the following weeks, trying to go to lunch with somebody new after every service. As I got to know these people, I was amazed at how genuine and real they were. I saw couples who talked about their love for their same-sex partner or spouse and their love for God in the same context without any conflict in between. It was the most beautiful thing I'd ever seen. Some of the couples I met had been together for ten, fifteen, even twenty-five years. Seeing their love for God and their love for each other normalized these two seemingly opposing worlds and married them in a way that I'd previously been unable to join together. It was what my heart ached for—to know it was possible to both love God and love a person who didn't fit the heteronormative narrative I'd been taught was required. I was seeing it with my own eyes, and it was captivating. In spite of how they'd struggled to get where they were, or perhaps because of it, they were the most humble, authentic, raw, honest, and genuine group of people I'd ever met. They gave me the courage to turn the corner and start accepting myself for who I was.

Although I was well on my way, before I could fully embrace myself, I still needed to examine on my own what the Bible really said about queer relationships. I asked

around and was given the names of a few books. I read
What the Bible Really Says about Homosexuality by Daniel
A. Helminiak. Though somewhat academic in its approach,
it walked me through each of the "clobber passages" (the
verses in the Bible that are believed to reference same-sex
behavior or relationships) with an unbiased lens, giving a
historical and cultural background to the verses and placing
them in the context of the times in which they were written.
It provided me with the knowledge I needed to wrap my
brain around what my heart was already finding to be true.

Unfortunately, books by affirming Christian leaders were still largely unavailable at the time; the LGBTQ+
Christian movement hadn't quite picked up enough steam
yet to really get off the ground. Resources have significantly
expanded over the last ten to fifteen years. I consider Colby
Martin's *UnClobber*, Kathy Baldock's *Walking the Bridgeless Canyon*, and David Gushee's *Changing Our Mind* to
be some of the best resources we currently have for decon-
structing theology in relation to the clobber passages. I also
didn't have access to any affirming memoirs by queer Christians at that time; again, this is something that has changed
dramatically over the last decade.* But books like *It Gets
Better* by Dan Savage and Terry Miller provided stories of
other LGBTQ+ people from all walks of life and helped me
find peace. My head and my heart began to unite.

The knowledge I'd gained through reading and research,
combined with the way I was experiencing faith and God
with other LGBTQ+ Christians and straight allies at my new
church, made me realize I had a decision to make: I could
wither away in a life of fear and shame and condemnation,

*See the Recommended Resources at the end of this book.

or I could live a life of truly trusting God. The kind of trust that was required of me to truly accept myself was a depth of trust I'd never known before.

It became clear that no amount of works or good deeds or prayer was going to make me straight. Being gay was as much a part of my identity as my brown eyes and big-boned frame. So all I could do was accept it and trust that living a life of authenticity would bring benefits that I couldn't yet see from the place I currently stood. I had to trust that I wasn't a mistake, that I wasn't inherently flawed, and that I was worthy of love and belonging.

I also had to look at the fruit my life was producing. Prior to accepting myself, I was filled with such self-loathing, fear, and shame that I considered ending my life. Trying to hide or change or fix who I was at my core was rotting away the best parts of me. Now, even though I remained terrified of what lay ahead, I felt free and full of joy, acceptance, wholeness, and peace. While the fear of being tormented for all eternity because of a characteristic I couldn't alter did cause me great trepidation due to the heavy emphasis evangelicals put on the afterlife, I had to come to terms with the fact that the hell I was experiencing on earth was a much more immediate threat.

I looked toward a future that was totally contradictory to what I'd been taught my entire life to believe. With two completely opposing views of the Bible's stance toward queer relationships, how was I ever to know for sure which is truly right?

For me, it came down to the simple yet difficult act of trust. I had to make a conscious decision to trust that God is a God of love, not a God of hate. A God of compassion, not a God of judgment. A God of expansive creativity and diversity, not a God of religious rules and tiny boxes.

A God of inclusion, not a God of exclusion. And I had to bathe in that and trust it *every single day.*

Coming to terms with this need for trust and accepting myself for who I really am finally set my soul at rest. Feelings of doubt were lifted, and I experienced a deep inner peace. My faith became more authentic and more genuine than it had ever been. For the first time, my faith wasn't about impressing God, or pleasing God, or putting on a good show for God to earn God's favor; it was based on trust and self-acceptance. It was centered in love rather than striving for perfection.

With this newfound peace taking root in my soul, I began settling into myself. I recognized myself as part of the LGBTQ+ community and slowly started identifying myself as gay. It was a new world for me, but one that felt right and good and free.

I remember the very first time I prayed for my future spouse as a woman rather than as a man. Excitement bubbled in my spirit in the place that guilt and shame once resided. The conflict I had once felt inside was disintegrating.

Still, I feared what was to come. I started confiding in a few friends and coming out to those I felt were the safest—mainly acquaintances. I figured the stakes were low and if it didn't go well, it wouldn't really matter. My Wiccan neighbor was thrilled that I was finally breaking out of the confines of my religion. My best friend from college was supportive and behind me all the way. A couple of coworkers even told me that this didn't come as a surprise to them. They'd known and were just waiting for me to tell them. It baffled me that someone else could know I was gay before I even knew myself. But they did, and were just patiently waiting for me to share this part of me with them.

Once I had a few positive coming-out experiences behind me, I moved down the list of who I needed to tell next. I was playing my cards very strategically and made sure to not tell anyone who knew my parents before I was ready to tell my parents myself. I didn't want to put anyone in the awkward position of having to keep a secret, nor did I want my parents to hear it from anyone other than me. I wanted to make sure it came from me first. I felt I owed them that much.

I did choose one of our close family friends who I felt deserved to hear it from me, and who I knew would also be a great source of support for my mom once I'd come out to my family. Her name was Betsy. I didn't know how my parents would react when I told them, but I knew the time to tell them was coming, and when it did, they were going to need support. So I told Betsy I had something important to tell her and asked if she would come to my house for a visit. She sat and listened graciously as I fumbled over my words, trying to get to the point of why I'd asked her to come. When I finally got out the words that I was gay, she calmly asked a few questions: *When are you planning to tell your parents? Do they have any idea? How do you know that God is okay with this?*

I struggled to explain the peace I'd found. It was a bumpy conversation, but Betsy was kind and loving, despite whatever personal feelings she had, and tried to reassure me that she loved me, my parents loved me, and everything was going to be okay.

I breathed a sigh of relief when the conversation was over. Betsy's family had been very close family friends of ours for many years. I taught her daughter piano lessons; we shared in holidays and celebrations together. I was grateful that one of the more difficult conversations was over and that it had seemed to go fairly well. I began to think maybe things would turn out okay after all.

But two days later, Betsy called. She asked if she could come back to my place again, saying she needed to talk to me. A nervous ball formed in the pit of my stomach. *Does she just have more questions? Or is there something more serious going on?*

When she walked in the door of my apartment, I could see she was troubled. Torn between her love and concern for me as a friend, and her respect for her husband, she sadly told me that she was pulling her daughter from piano lessons with me. She admitted she didn't understand the struggle I was going through but explained that her husband firmly believed it was a matter of spiritual warfare and that they could no longer allow their daughter to be under my influence.

Her daughter, who was a joy to teach, never showed up at my home for lessons again. In fact, I never even saw her again. Just as I feared, I was viewed as a spiritual deviant. Even worse, the labels so often assigned to gay people—that they are perverts, child molesters, and pedophiles—were now being applied to *me*. Labels were the very thing I was trying to break free of. Yet once again, they were being forced upon me. And these labels were the worst ones of all. They were more than devastating. They were dehumanizing. My heart was broken.

This was my first glimpse into what my life was about to look like once I came out to those closest to me. This wasn't sunshine and rainbows. This wasn't an exciting piece of news I got the privilege of announcing to everyone. This was heavy, and this was real. This was my life, and it was about to unravel.

I knew that I couldn't wait much longer before telling my parents. Whatever the outcome, my family needed to know. Now that my heart and head were finally aligned and no longer at war with each other, I couldn't keep it a secret any longer. I didn't want to live a double life. I was exhausted by having to filter everything I said around my family in order to keep them comfortable. I was sick of having to watch my words out of fear that they would find out before I was ready. Putting on a show was taxing on my brain and draining for my soul. I couldn't deal with that pressure anymore. There was no reason to wait any longer. Whatever their reaction was going to be, I had to do this. I owed it to them to tell them the truth, and I owed it to myself to be free from trying to uphold their unrealistic expectations of me. I could feel inside my spirit that the time to tell my parents I was gay was coming very soon.

Chapter 12

THE DAY EVERYTHING
CHANGED

The year before I came out to my family, I found a photograph of a man who had strung a tightrope across Niagara Falls from one side to the other. He frequently walked the tightrope back and forth, pushing a wheelbarrow in front of him. He asked an onlooker who stopped to watch, "Do you think I can do it?"

"I know you can do it," replied the man. "I've seen you do it a dozen times."

The tightrope walker responded, "Then get in the wheelbarrow."

I kept that picture taped to my fridge for an entire year before coming out to my family. It haunted me daily, posing the question, Do I trust God enough to metaphorically get in the wheelbarrow and come out to my family?

Nothing was more terrifying.

In the weeks leading up to my coming out, I was both excited to be free from the weight I'd silently carried and deeply anxious about how this would affect my relationship with my family. I didn't know what to expect or how they would react. I knew they wouldn't agree or be happy for me, but I didn't have a good gauge for how positive or negative their reaction would be. Anything from simply disagreeing but choosing to overlook it, to completely abandoning me and cutting me out of the family, was feasible. I knew the latter was the more extreme possibility, but I never thought that it would actually happen.

I'd always struggled to feel safe sharing my emotions with my parents, but even so, we were still a tight-knit family. We gathered for movie nights and pizza, we celebrated birthdays and spent holidays together, and on Christmas Eve, I still stayed the night at my parents' house so we could all wake up under the same roof on Christmas morning. We were there to help each other move, to see each other through medical procedures, and to enjoy family vacations in the mountains. Our family unit was strong. Even if our relationships functioned on a superficial level, there was still an expectation of showing up and spending time with one another. Coming out would definitely affect those interactions.

I knew it wouldn't be easy for my parents to accept that I was gay. It was going to take them some time to process and get on board. But considering our family dynamics, the way we were always present for each other's big (and small) victories, and the values my mom taught us growing up that family was more important than anything, I didn't expect my coming out to be as extreme as some of the horror stories I'd heard of kids getting thrown out of the house and completely disowned. Instead, I reflected on the phrase my mom frequently told us as kids: "Amber, friends will come and go, but your family will always be there for you." I clung to that and hoped it was true, because I knew family life was about to get tough.

Still, I was nervous as hell. Like a film in constant repeat, my mind flashed through the range of things that *could* happen, playing scenes of all the possible outcomes. The tension mounted to the point that not knowing how my family would react was causing more anxiety than actually knowing, and I couldn't handle it anymore. I wanted to get it over with so I could sleep at night without the daunt-ing uncertainty of what was to come.

I thought long and hard about the best time and place to tell them. I didn't want it to be during a holiday or birth-day celebration because if it went poorly, it would mark that holiday forever. I didn't want to steal joy from another fam-ily member's special event by dropping the l-word like an f-bomb in the middle of Thanksgiving dinner (which also would have been shocking, but more forgivable). I wanted it to be planned, thought-out, and purposeful. I didn't want to be impulsive and regret it later. Finally, when I knew I was ready, I told myself that the next time my brother was in town (he had moved out of state as part of a church plant), I would get the family together and tell them.

As soon as I made that promise to myself, my brother told me he was coming for a visit in just a few weeks. The moment I dreaded was suddenly upon me. I tried not to panic, but I couldn't help it. I had no idea what this was going to mean for my life and my future.

Not long before I came out, my dad and I enjoyed a special evening together and attended a wine tasting. Alcohol was completely forbidden in our house when we were kids, but once Daniel and I were grown, Mom loos-ened the reins a bit and Dad occasionally enjoyed a glass of wine. The evening of our wine tasting was close enough to my coming out that I already harbored anxiety of what my future relationship with my dad would look like. I remem-ber considering the worst and thinking, "This could be the last time my dad and I ever do something like this together."
Little did I know it actually would be.

The week before my brother came to visit, I sat staring at my phone for an hour before finally mustering the courage to call my mom. I picked up my landline phone, listened to the dial tone, and hung up. I tried again, listening to the dial tone a bit longer, and hung up again. Finally, I entered the home phone number and paused before hitting the final digit, knowing that doing so would connect the call. When I finally hit the button, my stomach quivered as I listened to the call ring through. My mom answered on the other end. "Hi, Mom, how are you?" I started, urging my voice to sound as normal as possible. I tried to carry on a nonchalant conversation with small talk like it was any other day.

Finally, when there was a break, I said, "Mom, there's something I'd like to talk to you, Dad, and Daniel about." Trying to come across as more confident than I actually felt, I continued, "I've been in counseling this past year working through some things, and I'd like to share some of my journey with you all. Would the three of you be willing to come to my house together this Saturday morning?"

My mom listened and hesitantly agreed to my vague request. Before I hung up, I let her know that my counselor had agreed to be there as well to answer any questions they might have, then quickly ended the conversation. After I hung up the phone, I exhaled a long, slow breath. It was set. April 14, 2012, was the day I would come out to my family. There was no going back now.

I spoke with some of my affirming friends and made plans for them to sweep me away to Denver for a "coming-out celebration" after the conversation with my family was over. I didn't know what was about to happen, but I knew that regardless of the outcome I would need to get away, have some fun, and get my mind off things. I hoped the celebration would be an antidote to whatever happened and infuse at least a small splash of joy for taking such a bold step toward embracing who I was.

As Saturday approached, I was edgy, irritable, anxious, restless, and terrified. Friends and even people I barely knew from my new church kept telling me I was brave to do what I was doing. But I didn't feel brave. In fact, I'd never felt more afraid of anything in my whole life. The fear was like a crushing weight on my chest that left me begging for air.

My heart pounded like drums in my ears the morning of April 14 as I prepared for my family to arrive. I dressed up a little, so as to appear more confident than I actually felt. I wanted to present a calm but assertive approach to the conversation. I knew that if I left the door open for doubt, my family would see it as hope that I might change. I wanted them to know that I was resolute and at peace.

Putting on my favorite piece of jewelry to comfort me, I heard a knock at the door. It was Morgan. True to her word, she showed up early to support me and be there for the family meeting.

In the few minutes we had together, I asked Morgan not to leave me alone after my family left, no matter how things went down. If the conversation went badly, I didn't trust myself to stay safe. I didn't know what I might do. I asked her to stay until one of my friends arrived to drive me to Denver, and she agreed.

Then there was another knock on the door. My stomach dropped and came up to my throat at the same time. I looked at Morgan with nervous fear, swallowed the lump in my throat, and forced a smile.

"Good morning," I welcomed as calmly as I could, opening the door and inviting my family inside. Their good-morning remarks were colder than normal. They were distant, guarded, almost as if they'd been prepped for the conversation. They clearly knew something was up.

I served them tea from the kitchen, and they each took a seat on the couch across from me in the living room. Morgan sat quietly to the side—present, but not intrusive. Tension hung thick in the air.

Finally, after some very awkward small talk, I inhaled the deepest breath I could muster and began.

"Thank you for coming this morning. There's been a lot going on in my life for the past few years and I feel like I'm finally at a point where I'm ready to share a very intimate and personal part of myself with you. I've been in counseling with Morgan for over a year now and she's helped me make sense of a lot of things as I've navigated this journey. She offered to be here today for support.

"Mom and Dad, I'm sure you've noticed that I've been more distant from both of you lately. That's because I wanted to search out answers for myself before sharing details with you. And now that I have, I want to catch you up. It takes a lot of courage to be this vulnerable, so I'm asking that you please hear me out."

All three of them looked frozen in their discomfort, lined up next to one another on the couch like sitting ducks. I glanced down at my notes, in hopes that it would give me strength. Then, forcing another deep breath, I started with some backstory.

"I know you're aware of what happened between Brooke and me several years ago, but a lot has happened since then. . . ."

I explained my journey and all that had transpired since Brooke had left. I spoke of the tremendous amount of condemnation, judgment, self-hatred, and shame I'd suffered; how I felt so suffocated inside that it caused me to relapse into self-harm after almost five years of being harm-free. I was open and vulnerable, exposing as much of my heart as I felt safe to, in order to help them understand the long road I had traveled. I talked about dating men, I told them about my time with Darius (leaving out that we slept together, of course), and I awkwardly told them about the woman I'd seen, trying to push past the obvious discomfort of sharing those words aloud with my own parents. I could see their level of distress deepening, but there was no turning back now.

I reserved using the word "gay" until the end, knowing that once that word escaped my lips, they likely wouldn't hear anything else I had to say.

"I've tried to change, but I *can't*," I explained. Not wanting to appear weak, I continued. "I got to the point where I couldn't deny my attraction to women, so I decided to face it head-on. I heard too many horror stories of people who suppressed their feelings and got married to someone of the opposite sex, hoping how they felt would just go away. Their marriages resulted in divorce because they couldn't escape the truth of their sexual orientation. But by then, so many more people were affected. I refused to let that be me and forced myself to look this in the face."

Blank looks of growing discomfort and concern continued to stare back at me, but I pushed on. I explained the research and studying I'd done, how I'd found a new church in Denver, the happiness and peace I'd found in the supportive community there, and finally, how I'd reached the conclusion that being attracted to someone of the same gender wasn't wrong or in opposition to God's will. Then, with all the courage I could muster, I pushed the two words out of my mouth that would forever change my future.

"I'm gay," I said. "I'm attracted to women, and I have been for a long time. I can't change it. It's part of who I am. And I can't pretend it's not anymore."

I assured them that this experience had only drawn me closer to God, not further away, and that I was in a place of peace—free of guilt and shame. I wanted them to feel reassured that my relationship with God was still intact, because I knew that would be their greatest concern. I explained that my close friends already knew, but that I hadn't told any other family yet out of respect for all of them. I wanted them to know first.

"I did already tell Betsy," I told my mom. "I felt she deserved to hear it from me herself and I knew she'd be a good source of support for you. Beyond that, you're free to tell or not tell whatever family or friends you want to. I'm not going make a big announcement of it, but I'm not going to hide anymore either.

"I don't expect you to agree or approve," I said. "I know it's taken me years to get to where I am and that it will take each of you time as well. But I love you enough to share this with you and not to hide it. I wanted to be honest and to let you know. I don't know what the future holds, but this is where I'm at. I'm gay and I'm at peace with that."

It is extremely disheartening to be in a room full of people and feel completely alone. But when those people in the room are your own family, the feeling is even more isolating. With my heart laid bare before them, I waited for them to respond.

Those few seconds of silence that hung in the air were the most vulnerable I'd ever felt in my life. My heart hung exposed and on display in front of my family, waiting to see whether I would be embraced or rejected. By the stoic looks on their faces, my hope for acceptance was quickly waning.

The first words to break the silence were in my mom's stern voice. "I don't approve of your lifestyle, Amber. Thank you for being honest with us, but we'll have to see what this means for the future of our family."

I tried to maintain my composure. *The future of our family?* What was *that* supposed to mean? I looked at my dad with hopeful apprehension. Finally, with pursed lips he said, "I have *nothing* to say to you right now." Turning to my mom, he informed her, "I'm ready to go," and stood to leave.

"I love you, Dad," I said, looking at him despondently, as if begging to hear those words reciprocated. But without daring to even look at me, his only reply was, "Thanks for the tea," and he walked out the door.

Once both my parents were outside, my brother and I were left together in the room. He came over, gave me a hug, and said, "I love you, Am." Then he too disappeared. And that was it.

The sound of that door shutting behind them as they left felt like they were simultaneously slamming the door of my heart that I'd opened to them. Frozen in shock, I looked blankly at Morgan, and then, in despair, collapsed into the chair behind me.

Chapter 13
BECOMING AN ORPHAN

Sitting with my head in my hands, I was devastated. I felt shattered inside, unloved and unlovable. I felt disowned. I felt rejected, and I knew there was no going back. It was my worst nightmare come to life, and I desperately wanted to wake up. I wanted to be alone so I could fall apart. But true to her word, Morgan wouldn't leave until we knew one of my friends was on their way to get me.

Looking back, if I could do it differently, I probably would. I thought that I owed it to my parents to come out to them in person. I thought they deserved to hear it from me, and that telling them in person was more respectful and honest somehow. But after being out for more than a decade and spending the majority of that decade living with and managing chronic illness and invisible disability, I see things differently. While I'll share more about the development of my illness in a later chapter, my experiences both as a queer person and as someone who is disabled have taught me a lot about healthy boundaries.

Years of people-pleasing, self-sacrifice for the sake of others, and striving to always follow the rules to the letter of the law have cost me a lot. My emotional, physical, and mental health have all paid a toll. Believing that people deserved things a certain way and always thinking of others before myself caused self-neglect, overextension of self, and the inability to ask for or even know what I needed in many situations. Doing what was best for others meant that I took on the penalty or absorbed the cost so that they didn't have to. That is not good self-care. Time has shown me that I am the only one who has to live with me for the rest of my life, so I need to take care of myself and make my body my friend. I don't actually owe anybody anything, and I am the one who has to live with the consequences of not setting healthy boundaries.

If I had done what was best for me, I would have written my parents a letter instead. It wouldn't have changed their reaction, but it would have shielded me from it. It also would have taken a huge amount of stress off my mind and body to have the opportunity to write my thoughts and feelings out on paper, instead of forcing myself to say the words to their face. One thing I've learned is that protecting myself is more important than protecting my parents. A child shouldn't have to shield their own parents from the truth. For far too long, I protected them (and their reputation) to the detriment of my own safety and mental health. But in the end, it didn't change anything.

The look on their faces the day I came out to them is forever seared into my memory, and in the weeks that followed I gathered many more snapshots that are still stored in the filing folders of my mind. I wish I had fewer of them. Even after all the years that have passed since that day, those memories are still painful to recall. The sting never quite fades.

But I did what I thought was best at the time, and now I had to live with the repercussions. I felt suffocated, and I was desperate to get away from it all as I anxiously waited for my friends to arrive and take me to Denver.

I went to a coming-out "celebration" of sorts that evening, though what I was celebrating I didn't really know.

People I'd never even met came to show their support. Many, with similar struggles of coming out, consoled me with statements like, "It just takes time. Your parents will come around eventually." I hoped they were right. Even though everyone kept telling me how brave I was to come out to my parents the way I did, all I could think of was how horribly wrong it had all gone, and how my life would never be the same.

We spent the night at a hotel in Denver, and the next morning, my friends dropped me off to the emptiness of my own apartment. Now that the distraction of "celebrating" was over, reality started to set in. I felt thoroughly depressed and wished I could just disappear. In retrospect, *that* is probably when I shouldn't have been left alone.

What I ended up loving even more than the coming-out celebration that night was a coming-out scrapbook one of my friends made for me as a form of encouragement. She and I collaborated to gather notes and pictures from everyone in my life who affirmed and celebrated all of me, and we pasted them into the book. It was a brilliant idea that ended up giving me strength in the months to come. Any time I needed reminding that I was loved just the way I am, I would sit on the floor, open up that scrapbook, and read all the encouraging notes my friends had written me. It comforted me for months.

After seven long days of silence from my family, I received a phone call from my dad.

"Your mom and I aren't ready to speak to you yet, Amber," he said in a firm tone. "But I just wanted to let you know that you're no longer welcome to go to the conference in St. Paul with your mom next month. I know you've already paid for your plane ticket, and if you still want to visit your friend there, that's up to you. But you can't stay with Mom at the hotel or attend the conference with her. And if you do decide to still go, you'll have to find someone else to watch your dog, because I won't do it. We'll let you know when we're ready to talk to you about this. Goodbye." And he hung up.

If I wasn't second-guessing my decision to come out before, I definitely was now. I'd hoped that they just needed some time to process what I told them—that they'd think about what I said and realize how much courage it took to share with them. I'd hoped that they would see how thoughtful and meticulous I was in my process and how important my faith still was to me. But now, it wasn't looking that way. I vacillated, wondering if I'd done the right thing. Maybe I shouldn't have told them after all. Maybe wearing a mask *was* easier than telling the truth. Maybe hiding *was* easier than being seen. But deep down I knew that the stress and exhaustion I felt from filtering everything I said in their presence was too much to stand long-term.

A life in disguise just isn't sustainable. It comes at a cost. It had already come at a cost. By compartmentalizing, not allowing myself to feel, turning off my emotions and desires, and trying to conform who I was to fit the mold expected of me, I made others happy but paid the price of self-hatred, self-harm, shame, and feeling like, at my very core, I was unworthy of love and belonging. That price—the price of my mental and emotional well-being—was too high, and I wasn't willing to pay it any longer. Living openly and honestly comes with a cost too, though, and I was about to find out just how much I had to pay for it.

It was three weeks before my parents contacted me again, telling me they were finally ready to talk. Although it made me uncomfortable, I agreed to meet them at their house, rather than in public, so we could talk more privately. Settling into the family room in the basement that held so many fond memories for me, it was clear that this conversation wouldn't be one of them.

My mom and dad sat side by side, presenting a strong, unified force. They prefaced the conversation with "Before we say anything, Amber, you need to know that we love you, but . . . ," and so it began. Couching harmful words and opinions with "I love you" does even more damage than simply saying the harmful thing. It communicates that love gives someone the authority or the right to say harmful things without feeling guilty for their words or responsible for their actions—like a free pass. "I love you, but . . ." is a common tactic to convince someone they are wrong about something but "because you love them" you have the right to manipulate their behavior into something that is acceptable to you. That is *not* love. The theory of tough love is a common one among Christians, and James Dobson's robust support of that theory influenced my parents a great deal. My parents had always looked to Dobson for advice, and they used his teachings to shape their response to me.

Dobson has written, "We are obligated as Christians to treat homosexuals respectfully and with dignity, but we are also to oppose, with all vigor, the radical changes they hope to impose on the nation. It is vitally important that we do so."[1] In the same article, which is full of nonsensical writing painting Christians as the victims of hate from "homosexual activists," Dobson denies having ever done or said anything that would be harmful to the LGBTQ+ community. Yet encouragement from evangelical leaders to implement a tough-love approach has been severely detrimental to many LGBTQ+ people, causing them to feel as if they have to change an innate part of themselves in order to be acceptable to their family, loved ones, and God. "Speaking the truth in love" is often used as a free pass that allows Christians to say whatever they want. As a result, it has driven many away not only from the church, but from faith altogether.

That's what my parents were about to do: "speak the truth to me in love."

"I feel like you've died, Amber—like I've lost you," my dad began with a grave look on his face. My mom agreed.

"I feel the same way. You've turned your back on God and everything we've ever taught you," she stated with resolve. Everything I'd told them three weeks ago about how much time I spent seeking God and researching the Bible, everything I'd said about how this whole process actually brought me closer to God, not further away, had been disregarded. They only heard what they wanted to hear.

"We're hurt that you didn't come to us with this sooner," my dad continued. "We would have loved to help you by sending you to a Love Won Out conference.* We would have loved to walk through this with you. Even if you still arrived at the same decision, at least we would have known that we did everything we could to persuade you. But because you didn't include us in your journey, it's too late. You've already made up your mind.

"But you're deeply deceived, Amber. Like Eve, you've eaten the fruit from Satan. You've gotten in with the wrong crowd and they've brainwashed you. You're putting your soul in jeopardy. I'm afraid that you're damning yourself to hell."

*Love Won Out was a conversion therapy ministry started by Focus on the Family and later sold to Exodus International.

Clearly their desire to "help me" was embedded in their desire to fix me and make me straight, or at least celibate. Their attempts to "persuade me" would have never ended, which is why I knew I had to appear resolute. Acting as if (and perhaps believing that) I had sold my soul to the devil, my dad went on to compare me to murderers, pedophiles, and bestiality.

"If I want to just go and marry a donkey, is that okay? Or if I see a little kid and want to have sex with them, can I just go ahead and do that and act on whatever I feel? You could even get a bunch of murderers together to form their own church and just make that all okay!"

Their words shattered me. I was devastated by their attacks on me, their own daughter, and felt gravely misunderstood. I didn't know what to say. I was tongue-tied and completely ill-equipped to handle such accusations. I never imagined I'd hear such horrific and violent words from my own parents.

As if pulling out her last resort, my mom stood up and walked across the room.

"I printed out the list of qualities you said you wanted in a husband," she said in a stern voice, throwing it at me. "Can you honestly tell me that if you found a man with all these qualities, you wouldn't fall in love with him?"

"I . . . I don't know," I stammered, feeling backed into a corner and trapped.

"I know," she shot back. "You would!"

"You don't understand," I tried. "This is not who I am. Do you want me to just be alone and miserable all my life?"

"I'd rather you be miserable in this life, than be miserable in the next," my dad retorted.

"We had no idea this was coming, Amber," my mom went on. "We honestly thought you were going to tell us that you had worked through all this and were over it. It's extremely selfish of you to do something that makes *you* happy without thinking about how this would affect the family." I couldn't believe she was serious. How this would affect the family is *all* I'd thought about for *months* leading up to this conversation. Why did they think I waited so long to tell them!?

"You've put your dad's job at Focus in jeopardy," she continued. "And your brother, at the happiest time in his life, now has to make decisions he should never have to make." My brother was recently engaged, so I can only assume she meant that he'd have to decide whether to include me in, or even invite me to, his upcoming wedding. It feels ironic that my mother would call me selfish for sharing something about myself that I had no control over, but not think my brother selfish for worrying about his wedding over my well-being and safety. Even more ironic since then is how many decisions I've been faced with that I never should have had to make—how many birthdays and holidays I've spent over the last decade without a single family member present, including my own wedding. Yet, she continued. . . .

"And your grandpa for years has looked forward to giving you his grandfather's pocket watch someday. But now, he can no longer do that because you're out from under his blessing. We can't do things to help you anymore, Amber. You've left our covering.

"Honestly, I don't know what holidays are going to look like in the future," she said flatly. "I don't know if you'll even feel comfortable being around us anymore." I think the reality was that they weren't sure if they would feel comfortable having *me* around for the holidays. Rather than seeing me as the same daughter they'd always known and loved, they now saw me as a prodigal daughter.

Then my dad added, "If you ever have a girlfriend, she'll *never* be allowed in our house. That's something that will never change. We're not going to disown or abandon you. We want you to know the door is always open, *if* you ever turn around and change." That word "if" is eerily similar to "but," coming with strings attached to their love and acceptance of me. These passive-aggressive comments and accusations from my parents were meant to guilt and shame me into repentance. It was clear that they were going to shun me to whatever degree necessary to make me change. That's when I realized that the unconditional love that they proclaimed to have for me all my life didn't really exist.

As their rebuke neared its end, my mom pulled out a book about a man who'd had "same-sex attractions"* but was supposedly healed through conversion therapy. She asked if I'd be willing to read it. I responded with what I thought was the best answer I'd given to anything all night, "Well, how about this? I'll read one of your books if you'll read one of mine?" offering what I thought was a fair compromise.

"No, I'm not interested in that!" my dad immediately shot back, without even the slightest consideration.

"Well, then," I said, "I'm sorry, but I'm not interested." I tried not to offend my mom. I even told her to let me know what she thought of it after she read it herself. But I let them know that I wasn't going to read it if they weren't willing to meet me halfway. It may have been the only strong response I had all night, but I was proud of myself for standing my ground.

---

*This term is in quotes because it is most commonly used by nonaffirming people and often associated with conversion therapy as something that needs to be fixed, changed, or healed.

Finally, after I'd been thoroughly reprimanded and ostracized, the conversation wrapped up. But as I went to leave, there was one final jab to my heart that made all of this very real. As I went to walk out the door, my dad asked for my key to their house. The childhood home that I'd grown up in from the age of seven, the door that had always been open to me to come by whenever I needed was now locked, and I was left out in the cold. I was now an outsider, no longer welcome as part of the family. He said they no longer trusted me to have open access to their home.

Baffled, I removed the key from my key chain and handed it to him. I think he tried to soften the blow by saying "I love you" before closing the door, but I don't remember for sure. All I could feel was the hurt, the pain, and the rejection from those I cared about the most. I never expected my parents to be accepting or approve of the fact that I was gay, but for the first time in my adult life I took the risk of completely trusting in their love for me as my parents, and was met with rejection. In my hour of greatest need, my family abandoned me.

Arriving home, I opened my journal and in utter heartbreak wrote ten of the most painful words of my life: *My worst fear has come true: I've become an orphan.*

I didn't know how my life would play out, but one thing was becoming clear. If I wanted to survive, I needed to move away from Colorado Springs.

Chapter 14

THE DEADLY EFFECTS
OF TOXIC THEOLOGY

My phone rang unexpectedly, pulling me out of the only work assignment I'd taken for the last week and a half. I quickly excused myself and ran to the hallway where I could take the call. It was my brother.

"Amber, something's wrong with Dad. You need to get back to the hospital immediately."

"Why? What's going on?" I asked in a panic.

"I don't know, but they're rushing him back in for emergency surgery. We need to get there fast!" he said, sounding equally anxious.

"I'm on my way!" I responded, hanging up the phone. I grabbed my things, quickly offered apologies to my coworkers through tears, and ran out the door.

That was the day I didn't know if I'd ever see my dad alive again. Only five months after I had come out to my family, we learned that my dad was gravely ill with a serious heart condition. Open-heart surgery was required as soon as possible. Daniel flew in from out of state and, regardless of the awkwardness I'd felt around my family since coming out, I drove down from Denver to be present for the operation. Daniel and I both agreed to put our differences aside and do anything necessary to help get our parents through this frightening and challenging time.

The surgery seemed successful at first, but as the week went on, Dad wasn't recovering the way we hoped he would, yet no one could figure out why. The doctors told us it might just take a little longer than predicted for him to heal. So one week post-op, they took him to run a series of tests before sending him home to finish his recovery. That's the day I decided to slip away for a few hours for a sign language interpreting assignment. It was the only time I'd left the hospital all week. Then I received the urgent call from my brother. The tests revealed what the problem was—and Dad could be within a few hours of losing his life.

By the time Daniel and I got back to the hospital, Dad was already being prepped for surgery again. Our fear was unspoken, but obvious—none of us thought Dad was strong enough to make it through surgery a second time. With heavy hearts, we all wondered if we'd see him alive again.

Once the nurse confirmed that he was back in surgery, we began the waiting process, just as we had done the week before. It was both surreal and uncomfortably familiar. In the quiet hours as we sat waiting for a verdict, I couldn't help but feel the weight of our strained relationship and all that had transpired between us.

A few months before, I had loaded up a moving van to start a new life in Denver. Taping up the final boxes, I could still hear the voices of my parents ringing in my ear.

"We would have loved to help you pick out a place and move to Denver, but because of *why* you're moving, we can't be involved."

"I know you think this is what's best for you, but I have lived a lot longer than you, and I can tell you, this will not end well."

"I'd rather you completely turn your back on God and be gay, than be gay and pretend like everything between you and God is okay."

Other repeated phrases, like, "The door is always open *if* you ever change," and "I love you, *but* . . . ," made it clear that their love for me, when tested, came with strings attached.

In time, they even tried to ask some leading questions, as FOTF advises.[1]

What led you to believe that you might be gay?
How long have you struggled with this?
Will you tell me again about the journey that you've been on?

But so much damage was already done that I was not able to open up and be vulnerable with them again. I didn't feel they were truly interested in my journey as much as they wanted to use the conversation as a gateway to help me change, or as my dad said, "fix things." My guard was up, my heart was broken, and I couldn't share any more with them until I felt like they were truly trying to understand me, without a hidden agenda.

I recognize that in many ways, my parents are victims of bad theology themselves. Shackled by fear in ways they may not even realize—fear of what God thinks, fear of what other people think, fear of losing their reputation or their job, fear of hell—they followed the guidelines of those in authority over them (who, again, spoke on God's behalf) and did what they believe God required or demanded of them. But my parents are not puppets. They are intelligent humans with the ability to think, to question, to research for themselves, and to choose. With the plethora of resources that have emerged over the last decade—incredible books, documentaries, and organizations all at their fingertips via the internet—there is no longer any excuse for their continued distance and silence. There is no excuse for ignorance when so much information is available. They intentionally choose to keep their blinders on and refuse to look beyond the realm that keeps them comfortable.

So many hurtful words followed behind me that day as I drove the moving truck from Colorado Springs to Denver, leaving my hometown behind. Twenty years of memories were built in Colorado Springs. My whole life had been shaped and molded there.

Driving north on I-25 on my way out of town, a new life now awaited me. I didn't know what the future held; I just knew my future was no longer in Colorado Springs. I'd lived there too long to walk around unnoticed. Now that I was out, I didn't want to ever have to hide who I was again. I couldn't handle the anxiety that accompanied the constant watching and wondering what other people were thinking. I needed to be somewhere safe, somewhere fresh and new, somewhere I didn't have to hide. So I left behind a world full of memories for an uncertain future, hoping to find a sense of normalcy and belonging again.

In the months leading up to my coming out, I made sure everything was in place for me to survive on my own financially, just in case the worst should happen. Even though I'd been living on my own for almost ten years, my family and I still shared things like cell phone and insurance plans. I was financially independent; however, being self-employed meant money was tight, and moving to a new city only compounded that.

I scrimped and saved any way I could just to get by. I turned down parties because I couldn't afford a gift. I turned down coffee dates with friends because I couldn't spare the gas to get there. I skipped groceries I could get by without. I even returned groceries to the store a few times. Money was tight, and once I came out, I no longer had family to fall back on in case of an emergency. With my bank account dwindling and my credit card approaching its limit, I hit bottom and found myself in tears the day I couldn't afford $1.98 for a half gallon of milk.

Living paycheck to meager paycheck, with only catastrophic health insurance in place, I was in a risky spot and had to trust my gut each day that I'd made the right choice for my future when I decided to come out. Some incredible friends stepped up for me during that period of transition and helped me find my new rhythm as I started my life over.

When I didn't have the full amount to put down on the condo I picked out in Denver, a member of my new church loaned me the advance with no questions asked. When I came down with pneumonia and kept willing myself to get better because I couldn't afford to go to the doctor, a choir friend handed me the needed cash and demanded I go. And when I desperately needed to learn and grow from a community of supportive Christians but couldn't afford the conference cost or travel fees, I was given a full-ride scholarship to attend. The generosity of my friends carried me through. Being forced to rely on other people, and even on my dog, to provide for my physical and emotional needs from day to day was humbling.

Still, living in a season of such uncertainty was frightening. I knew it would only take one thing going wrong to land me in a very dangerous and potentially homeless situation. In 2021, The Trevor Project conducted a study that found that 28 percent of "LGBTQ youth reported experiencing homelessness or housing instability at some

point in their lives."[2] Another study, from Chapin Hall at
the University of Chicago, found that LGBT young people
are 120 percent more likely to experience homelessness
than non-LGBT youth.[3] Most of these situations come as a
result of family rejection due to their LGBTQ+ status.

In the months leading up to and following my coming
out, my dog, Half Pint, became my closest friend. She was
an ever-present source of solace and support in the midst of
so much loss and pain. A loyal companion and comforter,
I gladly fed her before I fed myself. She was my one source
of joy and the one constant I could count on to be there and
love me unconditionally day after day. We bonded in a way
that only those who have grieved deeply could understand.

I felt as though so much of my life was out of my control,
and that's exactly how I was feeling again as I sat in the waiting room of the hospital—out of control. Although I was
sitting right next to my mom and brother, I felt alone. We
were joined together by fear of what was taking place in the
operating room, but my recent coming out set me apart. It
was painful to acknowledge that I was still there for them
even when they failed to be there for me. Although the four
of us as a family still shared the same blood, there was now
an obvious division between the three of them (Mom, Dad,
and Daniel) and me. Subtle cues in recent days made it
even more obvious, when my mom chose Daniel to be the
first to visit Dad in the post-op room after the initial surgery instead of me, or when we both arrived at their house
the day before the operation and she gave Daniel the newly
remodeled guest room (which used to be my room) and put
me on a blow-up mattress in the basement (where Daniel's
old room used to be). The message was clear: I was no longer equal to Daniel in their eyes.

THE DEADLY EFFECTS OF TOXIC THEOLOGY   167

Indirect manipulation and passive-aggressive behavior became the tactics my family chose in an attempt to get me to change. Rather than finding common ground in our love for one another as family, they silently punished me.

One of the most painful examples was when they planned an entire family vacation in the mountains without me and then invited me for only part of the trip. Despite the deep pain and exclusion I felt, I tried to remain steady and consistent. I wanted so much to prove to them that I was still the same daughter and sister they'd always had. So I decided to join them for a couple of days. But when I arrived, I was told to sleep on the pullout couch in the main living area instead of the extra bed that was available in the room where my future sister-in-law was staying. Their subtle actions over the next couple of days spoke volumes about how they felt and where they stood. Numerous times they quietly shunned me, pushing me further and further to the outside. I felt abandoned by those who promised they'd always love and be there for me. I felt like the family misfit, the black sheep, the outcast. It was one of the last times we ever spent together as a family.

My mom continued to make comments like "I know that deep down you know what you are doing is wrong" or "I have always spoken truth into your life and I will continue to do so, because I truly love you. It may not always be what you want to hear, but hearing the truth can be tough."

Although my dad and I weren't talking as often, his words sent in an email were equally painful, when he spoke of how embarrassed he was by me.

I could tell you that this isn't embarrassing Amber, but I'd be lying. It's very embarrassing. You made a choice that completely contradicts everything your mom and I taught you and know to be true. It stands opposite my life's work and the tenets of my employer. It is contrary to what Christians from the days of the first Church have held to be true. People look at me with certain expectations, and they have expectations that my family members will live according to the same principles that I've taught and believed. So I am troubled by the message this sends to hundreds of thousands of fans, and I am embarrassed by it. And this embarrassing situation hurts me. It hurts Mom, and it hurts everyone who has loved you and invested in you all these years. That it hurts you is sorrowful to me as well, but you made a conscious decision to pursue this lifestyle so you cannot blame us for the consequences of your choice.

These comments from my parents made it clear that if I wanted to feel loved, I had to play by their rules. And if I felt ostracized, it was my own fault—those are the consequences of sin. The fact that he couched the ending with another "I love you more than you know" didn't matter. Every "I love you" they spoke was drowned out by their hurtful words and shaming behavior. It was hard to accept that I was becoming so estranged from my own family when we'd once been so close.

But the proof that it was real sat in the awkwardness between us in the hospital waiting room, and in the ways I'd been treated since I'd been there. They were appreciative of my help. I don't think they expected me to come (which seemed absurd to me), so it surprised them that I was there supporting them for so long. Still, there was an obvious discomfort between us.

In the months since moving to Denver, I'd flourished in my new environment. I was finally appreciated and valued for who I was. It felt good to no longer live in my family's shadow. I was asked to be involved in leadership at church and joined a community choir where one of my original songs was performed and recorded in concert. Finally, people were seeing me for the gifts I brought to the table. Out from under the shadow of other people, I was able to let my own personality and talents shine.

But things were far from perfect. Friends were vanishing; many people who initially showed love and support grew distant or simply ghosted me over time. I wanted to fight to maintain each and every one of those relationships, but it became overwhelming. The silence I received from some stung just as much as the hurtful words I received from others.

A few people quietly observed my life from a distance long enough to see the positive light shine through. They saw me happy, they saw the joy I'd found, they saw how at peace I'd become. Although they didn't say much, I knew that by living my life openly and consistently in front of them, I was shifting their understanding of what it meant to be gay.

One day in 2016, I got an unexpected handwritten letter in the mail. It was from a friend and former coworker of mine. In the letter, she admitted that there was a mental barrier for her between continuing to be my friend knowing I was gay and continuing to be my friend once I married a woman. She apologized for not attending my wedding and spoke to the importance of unconditional love and bridge-building in the divisive times following the Trump election. The letter took so much courage and humility to write. It meant so much to know that by allowing this friend to quietly observe my life from the sidelines, I'd influenced her understanding and definition of love.

But then there were people, like my grandmother, who felt the need to take a more overt stand. On several occasions following my coming out, though she was pleasant and kind to my face, she followed up our visit with an email like this:

> In today's world Amber, it is very difficult to see a grandchild being deceived. We cannot twist Scripture to justify how we want to live. I know you well enough to know that in your heart, you know better than this. But I can tell that you are very determined to go ahead with it, even though not one single member of your family agrees with you. Satan always comes as an angel of light and you are letting a worldly view cheat you out of God's best for your life. God is a God of love and mercy and forgiveness, but He is also a God of wrath and punishment for disobedience.
>
> I love you Amber, but [there it was again, that "but"], I cannot condone what you are doing. If I didn't love you, I certainly would not speak so openly to you. I am concerned for your very soul. If this was of the Lord, it would not separate you from all those who love you and have invested in your life. You see, your family is always your family, but friends come and go.

I thought back to the countless times my mom had told me that very thing growing up: "Amber, friends will come and go, but your family will always be there for you."

I realize now that she'd learned that from her own mother. But as I looked around, I didn't see a single family member being there for me. Even as we waited for the results of my dad's unexpected surgery, my friends were the ones checking in, driving down from Denver to visit, and making sure I was okay. These friends were showing up for me, even as my blood relatives sat uncomfortably beside me.

After several hours went by, unable to wait any longer, Daniel went to the nurse's desk asking for an update. The nurse checked with the doctor and informed us that they were still in surgery, but that it shouldn't be much longer. I thought about the surgeon who was sewing up my dad's rib cage for the second time in a week. I prayed for him, and for Dad. I thought of how tender and painful the recovery would be if he survived.

It hadn't been long ago that I feared I myself might not survive. My depression was rapidly worsening and nightmares of how my family treated me invaded my sleep night after night. Often, it caused me to cry so hard in my sleep that I would wake myself up sobbing. This was the lowest point of my life. At every other turning point, there was always a light at the end of the tunnel that pushed me forward somehow. Always something that kept me going. But for the first time, I felt like that light had been completely extinguished. I couldn't see things getting better; I couldn't find hope, and as I searched for a reason to keep living, I could no longer find one. I felt consumed by hopelessness. Suicide was beginning to feel like my only real option.

I confided in my mom one day how suicidal I felt. Her emailed response was this:

I hope and pray you would never do something so self-ish, Amber. But let's look at this: you announce that you are gay, move away, choose to surround yourself with all new friends, family, and church members, knowing all along what we believe, what we stand for, and what our convictions are. And then it is our fault? That would be like Dad having an adulterous affair and then coming to me and saying that it's just who he is—he can't change, he is going to continue to have that affair, and I need to accept that. Then he tells me that he almost committed suicide because I couldn't accept the fact that he was living in adultery. Are you kidding me? You are NOT the victim here. If anyone has reason to feel desperate, it's me.

These are the most painful words my mom has ever spoken or written to me. She downplayed my pain, made light of my life's value, and made my sexual orientation equivalent to adultery. She ignored my cry for love and failed to recognize that their slow shunning of me is what was pushing me to the brink of suicide.

I began making end-of-life plans. Who could I trust to take care of my dog and faithful companion, Half Pint? Who would I leave my possessions to? I didn't have much, but my journals and scrapbooks had always been precious to me and held intimate pieces of my heart. I wondered who would care for them if I couldn't survive. My days were dark and long as I struggled with thoughts of death and wondered if I'd make it through.

There were so many moments when I wanted to give up on hope—days I was convinced that I couldn't continue if something didn't change. But for some reason, hope just wouldn't give up on me. In my lowest of low moments, I'd get a text from someone checking in to see how I was doing, or a church member would hug me in a way that showed they knew what I was feeling even without saying a word, or Half Pint would cuddle up right beside me as if to say, "Please don't leave me. I need you."

If I'm honest, it's Half Pint that saved my life. The connection and bond we shared was the only one I couldn't let go of. Half Pint was there when so many others walked out. Her unconditional love is what kept me going on my hardest and loneliest days. She was always excited to see me every time I walked through the door, and no matter what my day was like, she stayed by my side. We depended on each other to survive, and somehow, that was enough to carry me through when it seemed there was no other reason for living.

All three of us immediately stood in tense anticipation as we saw the surgeon, still in his scrubs, walking toward us.

"He's alive," the doctor said, hearing us collectively breathe a sigh of relief. "We drained ten liters of fluid from around his heart and lungs. He's very weak, but we found the root of the problem and the surgery was successful."

"Thank God," Mom whispered. "Can we see him?"

"He's in ICU and I want to keep him there for several days. You can see him, but only two at a time."

"Thank you, Doctor," Daniel said, offering a firm handshake.

"Yes, thank you," I chimed in. "You saved his life."

"It was a close call," the doctor replied. "If we hadn't caught it when we did, I don't think he would have made it through the day."

Tears welled in our eyes with the thought of how close we'd come to losing him, coupled with the relief of knowing he'd survived surgery a second time.

A couple hours later, I stood in the ICU room, holding my dad's hand. Still heavily sedated and on a ventilator, he wasn't alert, but I tried to let him to know I was there. Then, despite all the tubes he was connected to and all the machines that were aiding his recovery, he managed to find a way to send me a message. Coming as a surprise to me (it had been a long time since we'd used this secret code), he gently squeezed my hand three times. It was the silent signal we'd used all our lives to say, "I love you."

With tears in my eyes, I said, "I love you too, Dad," squeezing his hand in return.

Chapter 15

TURNING THE CORNER INTO DEEPER SELF-ACCEPTANCE

A full month passed before my dad was well enough to come home from the hospital. The doctors released him just ten days before my brother's wedding (which I *was* invited to but was given no role in). I wish I could say that my dad's near-death experience somehow changed his view of me and my sexuality, but it didn't. Of course, I didn't take care of him with the expectation that he would accept me, but I did hope during those weeks that my consistent presence might cause him to see me as the daughter he'd always known and prompt him to reevaluate what's truly important. But even as his frail body struggled to heal, his resolve was unchanged in his stance toward me. Once he arrived home, our relationship quickly returned to its awkward and distant state. It perplexes me how he could produce an entire radio drama documenting the life of Dietrich Bonhoeffer and yet fail to see the common threads of eugenics, marginalization, hate, persecution, and violence that weave through treatment of both the Jewish and LGBTQ+ communities.

I was disappointed and hurt, but not just with him. I was also disenchanted with the institution of the church and evangelical Christianity as a whole. I felt like they had failed me. In the time that I needed someone to love me the most, their tough-love approach taught my family and friends to distance themselves rather than embrace me. Their comfort took priority over my inclusion, and their fears won out over my need for love. The importance of family that FOTF taught; the value of community that the churches I attended growing up modeled; and our personal family motto, "Friends will come and go but family will always be there for you," disintegrated when I came out and left me feeling alone, even in the presence of family.

In my years of advocacy work, I've seen this story replicated in the lives of thousands of queer individuals and their families. Those with religious power have done a good job of instilling fear of LGBTQ+ people in those who subscribe to their spoon-fed theology. It's both disheartening and heartbreaking.

However, I've also seen a new movement rise up. The Mama Bears movement led by Liz Dyer and the Free Mom Hugs movement led by Sara Cunningham are rattling the system and calling parents to a better way—a way of fully loving and affirming their LGBTQ+ children. They teach, support, and educate parents on mental health statistics for queer people without family support. They go to pride parades and give out free mom hugs. They stand in at weddings where the couple's family has refused to attend. They spread and inspire love everywhere they go.

Starting with just over two hundred moms in 2014, the Mama Bears group has grown to more than thirty-six thousand moms and continues to rise with the release of the *Mama Bears* documentary by Daresha Kyi in 2022. While there are still a lot of stories like mine, there are also a lot of parents who are bucking the system, taking a verbal stand, and fully supporting their child, even at the cost of losing their own church, parental support, or friends. They are banding together to move the narrative toward love. It's one of the most hopeful shifts I see happening in our nation. These Mama Bears are a strong force, and they aim to change the institution that was built in hate against their LGBTQ+ kids. I've been the recipient of this Mama Bear love, and every time, it is powerful and deeply healing to me.

One of the hardest things for me to wrestle with in the years since coming out has been realizing that while many amazing parents *are* willing to take a stand and fight for their kids—my parents aren't among them. My parents still value their own comfort, reputation, and belief system over their own daughter. Even in the midst of the incredible support and resources that are now available, they choose not to fight for me—and that is perhaps the greatest wound of all.

So much took place within that first year of coming out—so many differing degrees of transition, grief, and loss. It's no surprise that my post-traumatic stress disorder (PTSD) significantly worsened during 2012. Every time I look back at all that year held for me, I wonder how I survived. Not only did I come out and move to Denver, but we also experienced the grave illness of my dad, my brother's wedding, and the unexpected passing of my favorite grandfather, Grandpa Henry. Being present for these life-altering events was not optional in my mind, yet they took a serious toll on me. So much was going on beneath my smile that other people couldn't see, and I was struggling to merely survive. I finally decided to speak with my doctor about training Half Pint to become a service dog. She had been instrumental in keeping me alive and aided my healing.

My medical records clearly indicated my long history of PTSD, and with all the additional trauma that 2012 had held for me, my doctor wholeheartedly approved. Half Pint immediately began training. She was overstimulated in public places at first, but soon she adjusted and was calm and content as long as I was near—like she was born for this role. The bond already formed between us made it easy for her to learn to recognize my anxiety and PTSD triggers. She wore her purple service vest with pride, knowing that putting it on meant she was working to help me. She regularly intervened to disrupt the PTSD cycle when it arose, bringing me back to a stable place.

I now realize that training Half Pint to be a service dog and moving to Denver were the two best decisions I made during that season. The ability to have a fresh start in a new city, combined with the support I found at my new church, and the unconditional love and assistance of Half Pint, are without a doubt what saved my life. I took small steps forward each day, doing the best I could with what I had, and eventually, a new year rolled in. I had never been so eager to mark the end of a year before. Thankfully, as I entered 2013, my life finally turned a corner.

In January 2013, I attended my first LGBTQ+ Christian conference. It was transformative. Hundreds of people from across the country traveled to Phoenix for the weekend to build community and gain a deeper understanding of what it means to live at the intersection of being queer and Christian. The room buzzed with excitement and camaraderie. There was a solidarity of experience and understanding among those present. So much love, freedom, and acceptance filled the room that my mind was on overload. The realization that there were so many other people like me was at once astounding, comforting, and deeply healing.

During the Q&A portion of one of the workshops, I made a comment about being the daughter of an FOTF employee and recently coming out as gay, and it caught the ears of one of the attendees in the room. Later that evening, he came up to me and said, "Hi, my name is Mark. This is my wife, Lynn. Can we take you to dinner?"

Surprised and a little perplexed by this invitation from a complete stranger, I wasn't sure what to think, but the uniqueness of this space and the safety I felt caused me to reply by saying, "Okay," followed by a smile. With little more information than that, I got in the car with a couple I'd never met and we headed out for a meal together.

Sitting around the table, an almost instant bond was formed as we shared our stories with one another. I told them about my upbringing as the daughter of a high-powered FOTF employee, about my coming out, and about the devastation I'd faced in recent months. They shared a very similar experience, but in reverse. They told me that two of their four daughters were gay, and that after ten years of struggle and estrangement from one of them, they were trying to embrace full inclusion and acceptance of their daughters.

Our willingness to be vulnerable in that space exposed an unrealized need that lay dormant inside each of us. I desperately needed to feel love and acceptance from a Christian parental figure. They needed a gay Christian "daughter" to learn from. Our need for each other fused our hearts and created a special bond.

Attending the conference that weekend was like crossing a threshold for me. In a way, it felt like coming home. Being surrounded by other queer Christians from varying backgrounds but with similar story threads was inspiring and healing, and it reduced the isolation I felt in my journey. I was encouraged by the stories I heard from the people who shared publicly about their shifts in theology. It further confirmed that I wasn't deceived the way so many family members and friends had said. I was hopeful because of the parents I'd met, like Mark and Lynn, that maybe someday things would get better for me too. It was a life-changing experience, and every time I see other queer people have a similar opportunity to be in an affirming space for the first time, it is equally inspiring.

I wish we didn't have to go away to an event to find this kind of experience. I wish this kind of safety just simply existed in our families, our churches, and our homes. Feeling safe to begin with is so much healthier than having to seek out safety in other places because our primal space isn't safe. Yet I'm so grateful that these spaces exist. Even ten years later in 2023, they're still very much needed. And each time I get to be in a room with "my people"—whether that is eight people or eight hundred people—it still feels like coming home.

Not long after attending the LGBTQ+ Christian conference that weekend, I woke up on a Sunday morning in February to a huge blizzard. The snow was deep, and I doubted whether I could even make it out of the parking lot, much less to the other side of town for church.

"Isn't this just my luck," I thought. "It would have to blizzard on the one day that I'm supposed to share *my* life story at church." Each week, my church had a preservice gathering similar to Sunday school, and once a month someone was chosen to share their story as a way of getting to know one another and better understand each other's journeys.

This morning was my turn. As if I weren't already nervous enough about sharing my personal struggles publicly to this group of church people, now I had to contend with three feet of snow. I was convinced I'd show up and see only four or five people sitting around one round table waiting to hear me—people who already knew my story because they'd walked it alongside me. Frustrated and a little bitter about the timing of this storm, I almost postponed my talk. But instead, I prepared myself for disappointment as I braved the icy roads.

Walking down the hall to the room where the gathering was held, I stepped through the doorway and stopped in my tracks. Before me sat a room full of people—people who cared about me so much that they'd shoveled their driveways, scraped off their cars, and driven to church in the snow just to hear my story. Overwhelmed by their support, I broke down in tears. I couldn't believe that so many people cared about me that much.

After taking a minute to collect myself, I began. I shared my growing-up years, passing around childhood photos for people to see varying versions of my cute three-year-old and seven-year-old self. I spoke of my journey through faith and sexuality and the turmoil I'd faced the previous year in light of coming out. And I took the opportunity to publicly thank many of them who had personally supported me in my journey along the way.

Sharing my story publicly for the first time since coming out was a powerful moment. It strengthened not only my confidence, but also my ability to live authentically in front of people, without hiding behind masks of perfection. It was freeing to finally show all of who I was in front of an audience, without parts of me being forced to silently hide from the public eye. To receive such love in return strengthened my ability to love myself and realize that there is space for all the pieces and parts of me to coexist together in unity.

Chapter 16
CHOOSING LOVE

There were two things my mom always told me about meeting the love of my life. The first was that meeting the right person often happens when you least expect it, and the second was that when you find the right person, the relationship can move along quickly. Both of those were true when I met Lyssa. We met at church in February 2013, and by April, we were dating. In many ways, this felt like my first real dating experience. I fell into my relationship with Brooke; it wasn't intentional. And the period of trying to figure out my sexuality consisted of only a handful of dates with a handful of people. This was my first time in a real dating relationship for any length of time.

It was a season of excitement, of falling in love, and of discovering new parts of who I was and what I had to give. It was also the first time I ever got to publicly introduce someone as my girlfriend. There was no more hiding or sneaking around or changing pronouns to mask that I was in a same-sex relationship. It was freeing and came with a level of joy that said things were finally the way they were meant to be.

I wanted so much to be able to share this new and exciting part of my life with my parents. I wanted to celebrate this season with them and for them to get to know

Lyssa. But sadly, the longer that Lyssa and I dated, the more my relationship with my parents eroded.

My dad told me that when it came to holidays, I would always be welcome in their home, but Lyssa would never be allowed under their roof. It was heartbreaking that we couldn't share holidays together as a family the way we once did, but going without Lyssa was never an option to me. I told him that saying she wasn't welcome was the same as saying that I'm not welcome. Putting it in perspective, I reminded him that he would certainly never go somewhere for the holidays where Mom wasn't allowed. My relationship with Lyssa was no different. This boundary was a hard one to set, but it felt obvious. It was about dignity and respect, both individually and as a couple. It was about being treated equally with my brother and his wife. And it was about prioritizing my relationship with Lyssa as my partner.

I believe that when you enter a serious committed relationship with someone, that person becomes your nuclear family and that relationship needs to be fostered and protected over your birth family, especially when complicated dynamics are in play. I never asked or expected my parents to agree with our relationship, but I did ask that they treat both me and Lyssa with respect, both as human beings and as adults. Yet they struggled to do that.

I tried to let go of my need for their approval, but it was hard. Their pride in my accomplishments had carried me through a good portion of my life. My people-pleasing nature wanted them to be proud of me for the milestones I was achieving—to praise me for all I had overcome, to be happy that I had finally found love. But ultimately, I realized that I had to release that deep longing and start setting boundaries with them in order to protect my own physical and emotional well-being.

Setting boundaries with my parents was not something I was used to. Honoring your father and mother was an important value in our home, and setting boundaries with them was considered disrespect. That meant it was just as hard for them to accept the boundaries I set as it was for me to set them. Although it was difficult, the longer that Lyssa and I knew each other, the more secure I felt in her love, and that love empowered me, over time, to refocus my priorities.

After eight months of dating, getting to know one another, laughing together, and creating memories of our own, Lyssa and I were engaged. While it seemed quick to some, we felt ready. We were both well into our adult lives, so, to us, there was no reason to prolong what we already knew we wanted.

It's true that to a degree, coming out is like going through a second adolescence—or for some, perhaps even a first one. Denied so many of the experiences that straight teens have, we feel delayed in our social and romantic discoveries. Because I was still newly out when Lyssa and I met, this season was exciting for me. Someone loved me and actually wanted to be with me. I suppose it also partially filled the emptiness I felt from losing my family. Those milestones and holidays that were void of family were now spent with Lyssa.

I didn't yet realize the degree to which purity culture was continuing to influence my life. There were blind spots I simply couldn't see in our relationship at the time due to the limited knowledge and dating experience I had. In many ways, I feel like I didn't really find myself or know who I was until several years into our relationship and marriage. This is common among those affected by purity culture, as well as queer people who come out later in life.

Putting the two together makes it twice as challenging. If I had known then what I know now, perhaps I would have made it a point to date more people and get to know myself better before committing to a long-term relationship. Rather than addressing some of my concerns, I ignored the feeling in my gut that detected a few red flags, and leaned into the consolation that no relationship is perfect and each one takes a degree of work to succeed. I did the best I could with the tools I had, and at the time, it seemed like what we had was mostly good, mostly loving, and mostly safe.

We started making announcements and planning for the big day. Excitement rose. Venues, dates, color schemes, the wedding party, and more all spun like a whirlwind. I planned endlessly. It had both its moments of euphoria and extreme stress. Anyone who's ever planned a wedding knows what I mean. It's utter chaos.

The daunting task of telling my parents we were engaged felt like the equivalent of a second coming-out. I knew that for them it would solidify what, up until that point, they'd hoped would still change. It took me so long to muster the courage to tell them that, sadly, they ended up being among the last to know. Joy was flourishing in my life, and I didn't want that joy to be smothered by further disapproval. I finally felt truly happy, and I wanted a chance to soak it up. But it made me sad that in order to feel happy about getting married, it meant not sharing that information with my parents. I wanted to be like straight couples who couldn't wait to tell their family and who immediately began dreaming and planning together.

Unfortunately, just as I feared, when I finally did tell my parents Lyssa and I were engaged, I received a ten-page letter from my mom detailing her heartbreak and despair over the direction my life had taken. She still believed that I had strayed from God and from everything they raised me to believe, and that with enough prayer, one day I would return to the foundation I was grounded in as a child. My mom made a point of telling me that she does not believe anyone is born gay:

> I believe something happens along the way to confuse or hurt them that makes them turn to homosexuality for the affection and love they so desire. I do not despise you or any gay person. I do despise Satan, who is a deceiver and is leading so many astray. But I also believe we serve an amazing God who forgives all of our sin, heals all of our diseases, and helps us gain victory over them.

I wish my parents didn't see me as confused and wounded. I wish they didn't see my relationship with Lyssa as sinful and diseased. Even amid all the hurt from rejection, there's a part of me that is sad for them—sad that they are unable to see God outside of the small box and set of rules so many Christians have forced God into. They have no idea that God's desire is to not only shatter that box, but to make the world even more beautiful with its vast array of diversity.

At the end of the letter my mom told me that she has an angel named Hope that holds a candle, and that it is sitting on her coffee table in honor of me. She said that every time she sees it, she prays for my return: a return to myself, to my family, to my friends and loved ones, and to my foundation. She vowed to always leave it there until I return to them and promised she would never give up hope. She'd pray that I'd return sooner rather than later, but regardless, will always be waiting for my return with open arms.

It hurts to read this because I will never "return to them" the way they hope I will. Even amid all the heartache and loss, I came alive the day I came out. I finally found myself and who I was meant to be. Once you've had that revelation and found the piece of you that was missing, there is no going back. To do so would be lethal.

I've also met my people. People who are raw, authentic, honest, and vulnerable—the kind of people I've been looking for all my life. You don't arrive there by accident. It takes intentional hard work and going through some tough shit to find that place of genuine and meaningful community. The people I've found are radically inclusive, eager to learn, and embrace God in all her beautiful and diverse forms. Yes, I just used a female pronoun for God. The reality is that God is beyond gender, and continually assigning masculine pronouns to God only reinforces patriarchal and misogynistic mind-sets. To embrace diversity, we must first dismantle the patriarchy. For many of us, that starts with the way we view God.

In addition to knowing that I would never return to my family in the way that they hoped for, I also realized that I was unwilling to ever go back to dismembering myself. Hiding important parts of me for the sake of appearances, denying the core of who I am, suppressing my identity, and parceling out only what is acceptable in a given situation was to kill myself repeatedly little by little until everything good about me was dead. That is not God's intention for us. Jesus came to give us life to the fullest extent possible.[1] With time, I've become strong enough in who I am that I refuse to ever wear a mask again in order to make other people comfortable, even when those people are family.

One of the hardest things I've ever had to do is plan my wedding, knowing that my family wouldn't be there. My parents refused to even meet Lyssa when we were dating. After learning that Lyssa and I were engaged, my mom made it clear that, at a time when she should be rejoicing, she was grieving. She was unable to share in the wedding-planning process because she could not go against her convictions and support the choices I was making.

"I want you to understand why," she said, as if I didn't already know. "I believe that God clearly lays out in the Bible that marriage is to be between one man and one woman. Marriage is a holy sacrament put in place by God to signify and represent the church as his bride. That is what the entire foundation of Christianity was built on and if we lose that, we lose everything. I love you, but sometimes love is very hard."

There are two things I learned from that statement. First, whether she realizes it or not, my mom is afraid—afraid that if she condoned my relationship with Lyssa, it would put a crack in her belief system that would spread, causing her entire foundation of faith to crumble. That fear is very real. I remember facing it myself and thinking, "If I'm wrong about *this*, what else am I wrong about?" It's terrifying to feel like the entire foundation you've built your life upon is being shaken. It takes incredible strength and courage to walk that path in faith, despite the trembling ground, and face that life-altering fear head-on.

The other thing that came through loud and clear in that statement was her belief that love must be tough and hard. And it *was* hard. The way they chose to love me was hard for me as well as for them. I recognize that being gay and marrying a woman is not the direction they saw my life going. I can even sympathize with the fact that it changed some of the dreams or expectations they had for me. It changed some of my dreams as well, not because my dreams themselves changed, but because they lacked my family's presence in them. The wonderful couple I met at the LGBTQ+ conference, Mark and Lynn, even offered to speak to my parents on my behalf. They wrote a beautiful letter telling them a little of their own journey with a gay daughter and offering to talk with them in more detail. But my dad turned them down flat. He said he already knew the truth about what God said on this topic and didn't care to discuss it further.

So I knew there was no way they would even consider attending my wedding. They would not let their presence show support for a commitment of love they saw as shameful. And yet, an invitation with their name and address sat on my kitchen table for weeks, as my broken heart so deeply wished that things were different. Everyone should have the love and support of their parents on their wedding day.

But instead of feeling supported, the thought of them being there caused me intense anxiety. Our relationship was so turbulent that I knew their presence would *not* be comforting. That realization was as painful as knowing they refused to have any part in our lives. Our wedding was a day I had looked forward to all my life. Lyssa and I were happy together. I felt whole and free. My heart ached and longed for my relationship with my parents to be in a place where they could celebrate that with us. But it was not.

Every time I thought about my parents attending our wedding, my anxiety mounted. Fear of my family showing up at the ceremony with intervention plans provoked nightmares unlike any I'd ever experienced. Deep sobs from intense heartache repeatedly woke me in the midnight hours. All through the coming-out process I tried hard never to lash out in anger, never to say things I might regret or that could be used against me. I tried to be calm but firm in the boundaries I set. I fought to maintain connection during holidays and birthdays, attempting to show them I was still the same person and that they were still important to me. But over time, it became exhausting and depleted my soul. The constant anticipation and wondering what to do for that birthday, or how to handle this holiday, drained me of all my emotional energy. It became toxic. I tried to keep a wall around my heart to prevent them from seeing how much damage they'd actually done, but in hindsight, I wish they had seen more of it.

In 2012, the year I came out, I worked hard to maintain contact with my family as much as possible and cultivate a sense of normalcy, but that waned in 2013 as Lyssa and I met and started dating. Conversations between my parents and me went from cold to icy. By the time Lyssa and I were engaged and planning our wedding, my relationship with my parents had disintegrated almost completely.

Eventually, I had to make the difficult decision to remove all family from my Facebook account. I'd fought against it for a long time. It felt like the last window I had into their lives. Ultimately, while that final string kept me connected to them, it also served as a constant and painful reminder that I no longer belonged. Posts showed up in my feed of holidays I should have been a part of, family vacations I should have been included in, and memories we should have shared. Each left me feeling more of an outcast from the family. My mom posted pride over her daughter-in-law and the time they spent together the way she previously bragged about me. I felt replaced, and it ate me up inside. I finally had to cut the tie and let it go.

Our conversations became less frequent as the wedding drew near. I didn't mention it. They didn't ask. But mostly, we just didn't talk. All the other areas of my life were so filled with joy. It angered me that family disagreements tainted this beautiful season. Ironically, the more distant our relationship became, the better I handled it. Not that it hurt any less, but having some room to breathe allowed me to begin healing.

Not long before ties were completely cut between me and my parents, I hit a point where I'd felt backed into a corner for so long that I finally wrote them a letter and told them how their comments and treatment affected me. I'd heard countless times of the ways I'd disappointed them, how embarrassed they were by me, and how my choices were sinful and putting my soul at risk. I owed it to them—and more importantly, to myself—to tell them the effects of their behavior.

I was respectful, but direct and honest. I no longer minced words. I knew it could come across as harsh, but I was no longer willing to absorb their hurtful words and say nothing. I deserved respect. I was tired of being bullied by my own family into believing and doing what they thought was right, and I called them on it. At the end of my letter, out of my deepest pain and anger, I told them, "If you love me, prove it—because right now, I don't believe you."

Those were the harshest words I'd ever spoken to my parents. But I needed them to know that what they perceived as love was really just an excuse for their bullying behavior.

As expected, everything I said fell on deaf ears. The only response I got to everything I expressed was, "I'm sorry you feel that way. I hope someday you will understand the reason for our decisions, and come to know how much we truly do love you."

That was one of the last times I ever spoke to my parents. It was only two months later that my dad drew a line in the sand, saying he was tired of the drama and couldn't handle the stress anymore. We haven't spoken since.

I married Lyssa in June of 2014 without a single family member present. Friends from our affirming faith community (and even a few strangers) showed up to support us and stand as placeholders where my family should have been. I now realize that it took a great deal of bravery to walk down the aisle that day, defying all the odds that said we didn't deserve to be together, or to be alive at all. The day was beautiful and (other than the obvious lack of family support) everything we dreamed it to be. Everyone deserves to have the day of their dreams. We made a decision to walk toward each other that day, and into the future of all that lay ahead.

PART 3

THE YEARS SINCE

Chapter 17

BEGINNING TO LIVE WITH CHRONIC ILLNESS

Starting the twenty-minute meditation on my Insight Timer app, I sat a bit uncomfortably, trying to relax as the woman's gentle voice guided me in how to connect with my body. Meditation was new and a bit foreign to me, but I was doing my best to lean into it, since my doctor informed me of how it could help relax my nervous system. A meditation specifically tailored to those with chronic illness, the woman's gentle voice started with a body scan to help each of the muscle groups relax. Then, continuing to gently lead, she went on to say, "If you have a disease or condition, say to it now, 'I love you.' Love is the only vibration that heals."

Fuck you, came my guttural reaction. My body was racked with dysfunction from the late-stage Lyme disease that had overtaken my health, rendering me frail and disabled. *How dare she tell me to love my sick body?* I retorted in anger. Oblivious to the outrage I was directing toward her through the app, she calmly continued, "Say to it, 'I accept you.' Whatever we accept can change, whatever we resist persists. Send love and acceptance to any illness or condition you have now. . . ." I started sobbing. Big tears ran down both sides of my face. I did *not* love this illness. I did *not* love my pain. I did *not* love that I had been diagnosed with one of the most intelligent and complicated diseases a person could contract—a disease without a cure.

Several years after coming out, the toxicity of existing in a constant state of turmoil, combined with the intense long-term stress my body had been under, created the perfect breeding ground for the *Borrelia burgdorferi* (the bacteria responsible for Lyme disease) that was lying dormant in my body to come to an active state. Though it progressed slowly at first, over time it infiltrated all the systems of my body, altering my ability to do a variety of basic life functions.

The body keeps the fucking score. Trauma isn't just something that happens *to* us, it happens *in* us. And our bodies remember.

My journey with chronic illness and pain began in 2013 when my mobility began changing. First, I started to limp, then I had difficulty going up stairs, then even walking became difficult. At twenty-nine years old, I started using a cane for support. Eventually I had several days when I couldn't even get out of bed on my own.

After I had waited months to see a doctor, the first doctor I did see told me to "put some ice on it and take Ibuprofen to see if that helps," as if I hadn't thought of that sometime in the past year while navigating the nightmare that is our health care system and watching my mobility decline. I requested an MRI. It was clear she thought that I was overreacting, but I stood my ground.

Upon receiving the results, they sent me to see the neurosurgeon who told me it appeared that there was a cyst on my spine, but that he didn't feel comfortable operating because the risk of paralyzing me was too high. He referred me to Anschutz Medical Campus—one of the top medical facilities in Denver. The doctor at Anschutz took one look at my MRI results and said, "Well, I'm not sure what's causing your pain, but you do *not* have a cyst on your spine. What your previous doctor saw is an ovarian cyst. He read the test upside-down."

Excuse me??? A neurosurgeon read my test upside-down??? That was it. I knew that day that I had to find a way out of this system and into the hands of someone who could actually help me. It took months (as navigating health care does), but I finally got in to see a doctor of osteopathic medicine, who instantly pinpointed the root of my pain.

"Does it hurt here?" he said, pressing on the sacro-iliac (SI) joint at the base of my spine. I winced, but felt so seen and validated in that moment. After multiple doctors had run multiple tests and passed me around, only to tell me, "We don't see anything wrong" and "It's all in your head," this doctor listened to and believed me.

We started an intense treatment right away, designed to help my ligaments regenerate and heal slowly over time. I did the treatment every other week, and it laid me up in bed for three to five days each time. It was miserable, causing fevers, body aches, and extreme fatigue, but I was desperate and willing to do anything to feel better.

I continued these treatments biweekly, then monthly for a couple of years, even transferring physicians midway when my first physician had to unexpectedly retire. Slowly, I began to see improvements and regain mobility . . . to a point. What I didn't know was that no one should ever have to do this treatment for the length of time that I had done it. Most people only needed about six to eight treatments to achieve full healing; I stopped counting somewhere after thirty.

Over time, though, I began clueing into the fact that there was something more going on in my body than just the loss of mobility from this chronic SI pain. While my mobility did improve with treatment, other symptoms started presenting themselves. I finally realized: something isn't right. My symptoms kept snowballing: excessive fatigue, susceptibility to infections, frequent fevers, shortness of breath, nerve tremors, brain fog, muscle weakness, memory loss, trouble with word recall, heart palpitations, heat intolerance, full-body crashes—the list got longer and longer.

I began working with a functional medicine doctor who was compassionate and full of care. She didn't just simply run lab work followed by "Everything looks fine!" She listened to what I was feeling and experiencing and continued to run layers of additional tests to search until we found the answer.

At some point along the way, a friend who had Lyme herself talked to me and urged me to consult my doctor to see if I might have Lyme disease. I was skeptical, yet desperate enough to do the research. What I found scared me—partly because the condition was so daunting and partly because it resonated so deeply. The next time I saw my functional medicine practitioner to review where we were and determine next steps, I gathered the courage to look her in the eye and ask, "Do you think this could this be Lyme disease?"

"Yes," she said without wavering. I took a long, slow breath, taking a moment to let it sink in.

"Okay," I responded, "what do we have to do to find out?"

She ran one of several imperfect and often unreliable tests for Lyme disease. The *Borrelia burgdorferi* bacteria associated with Lyme disease is a spirochete in class and is one of the most intelligent bacteria known, with the ability to camouflage itself to hide in the different systems of your body, thus at times rendering false negatives. However, for me, there was no hiding. My spirochete bacteria were out and actively spiraling the day I tested for Lyme disease. After multiple doctors, myriads of tests, and six years of helplessly watching my body decline, I was diagnosed with late-stage Lyme disease on June 19, 2020.

LGBTQ+ people are disproportionately affected by chronic illness and pain due to the extent of identity suppression, institutionalized prejudice, social stigma, hate, violence, and exclusion they experience. In fact, 21 percent of LGBT+ people report having a disability or chronic illness.[1] This is 50 percent higher than for those who do not identify as LGBT+. The degree of oppression and estrangement queer people face, both by loved ones and by society, puts their body in a constant state of "fight or flight." One can only maintain this for so long before the body begins to break down. *We aren't meant to live that way.* This is why living openly and honestly, setting healthy boundaries, and protecting our mental, emotional, spiritual, and physical well-being are so critical. Our health quite literally depends on it.

Lyme disease was not the diagnosis I wanted, yet I was relieved that I finally had an answer—a name and clinical proof for all that I had been feeling and experiencing for years. I was transferred to a Lyme-literate physician who took over my case. This physician informed me that while there is currently no cure for late-stage Lyme disease, there is hope for remission. We began treatment immediately.

We spent the entire first year after my diagnosis running a battery of tests to fully determine the severity of my case. My first lab draw was twenty-one vials of blood. Subsequent ones were in the teens. Some of the coinfections that came back negative on my initial test needed to be tested differently to see if they were truly negative or simply hiding in my body at the time of testing. This protocol consisted of treating the infection as if I had it, to see if it caused a Herxheimer reaction (a flare-up of all the symptoms); if it did, that meant I was positive for that infection. It felt like an endless loop of testing, herxing, getting my body back to a stable place, and then doing it all over again. It was mentally, emotionally, and physically exhausting. I came back with some of the highest inflammation markers my doctor had ever seen and tested positive during several of the herx tests that drew out other coinfections of Lyme in my body.

Learning, understanding, and advocating for myself while being so incredibly weak and ill was incredibly daunting, overwhelming, and, at times, debilitating. Because much of the Western medicine world does not yet recognize *chronic* Lyme disease, it becomes that much more difficult to gain access to resources, reliable knowledge, trained doctors, and treatment.[2] Not only that, but because it is largely unrecognized, it's not covered by insurance, making most, if not all, of the testing and treatment costs out-of-pocket expenses, including doctor's appointments (which are required every six to eight weeks at four hundred to eight hundred dollars an hour on average).[3] It makes it nearly impossible for someone with this condition to both work while they are so incredibly ill *and* pay for the host of medical expenses they regularly incur. The cost is overwhelming. The treatment is overwhelming. The symptoms are overwhelming. Putting this burden on a queer person who has already spent their whole life being resilient and defending their existence to the world can teeter on lethal.

Fiercely independent and determined not to be a burden, I pushed hard to keep up with my work, chores, responsibilities, and commitments even when my body begged and pleaded for rest. I'd wait to rest when no one was around so as not to be seen as lazy, even though at times I felt the need to go back to bed only an hour or two after waking up. Old tapes of productivity being tied to worth die hard. Some days I'd sit on the edge of the bathtub and cry because even simple things like taking a shower or brushing my teeth felt too hard. Often, I'd open the refrigerator looking for something to eat, stare blankly at my options, then close the door and walk away because the steps between the options I saw and actually getting food in my mouth felt too overwhelming. During a full Lyme crash, even lifting a spoon to my mouth can feel too heavy. There are days I simply don't have the energy for the most basic tasks, which means socializing has to come second. But sacrificing socialization for basic life needs is extremely isolating and has a drastic effect on one's mental health. So at times I hid the severity of my exhaustion from others, so as not to be excluded.

One of the most challenging things with Lyme (and many other autoimmune conditions) is that it fluctuates from day to day. You never know what amount of energy or symptoms you're going to wake up with each morning. It's always a gamble. It's easy for people to see me out and about and think, "But you don't *look* sick." That's because (a) I mask it well (remember, I was trained for this), and (b) you will only ever see me on my best days. If I'm flaring, I won't be out. If I'm traveling or speaking, I've planned for that. I've mitigated a number of obstacles to make it happen and planned strategically how my time and energy will be disbursed. That is why, if I arrive at a speaking engagement and suddenly the host wants to add an extra gathering or meet-and-greet, I often have to decline. It's not that I don't *want* to do those things, but rather, I've carefully planned my schedule in line with what my body is capable of doing without crashing, and to add to that could tip the scale, rendering me useless.

My body can still go from walking normally to needing a wheelchair in the span of a day if I'm not careful. Sometimes I get it right. Sometimes I get it wrong. Almost always I have recovery time on the back end. Life for anyone with Lyme is a hell of a lot.

In February 2023, I received an additional diagnosis, rheumatoid arthritis (RA). Different from osteoarthritis, RA is a chronic inflammatory autoimmune condition in which a person's immune system attacks the tissues in their body. Sitting with this new diagnosis in addition to Lyme has been hard and sobering, though it is not uncommon for these two conditions to couple up in one's body.

Everything in life now has to be at a slower and more flexible, simplified pace. This has been a big lesson in letting go of perfectionism and performance-based self-worth. It can make friendships and social commitments challenging, often causing me to feel like I'm slowing others down or holding them back. But I do have a small handful of people who take it upon themselves to assume responsibility as my friend and keep me safe by doing things like masking in crowds when with me (even if that's no longer their norm), thinking about seating that is comfortable for me at restaurants, or simply walking at a slower pace when my energy is low. Their love for me and concern for my health outweighs their need for comfort or speed. There aren't adequate words to describe what that means to me. All I can say is, it's love and inclusion at its finest.

Chapter 18
HOMETOWN PRIDE

Ten years after coming out to my family and moving away, I sat on the shady side of Tejon Street in downtown Colorado Springs waiting for the 2022 Pride Parade to begin. With hundreds of people lining the streets and a few beside me whom I considered chosen family, it felt like a redeeming moment for me. I was surprised by the turnout and amount of representation. It forced me to shift the lens through which I viewed my hometown.

About six months prior, I did something I never thought I'd do—I moved back to Colorado Springs. And as a single woman, no less. After marrying Lyssa in June 2014, we had a handful of mostly good years together. Then the pandemic hit, and we became a statistic.

I never thought it would happen to me. I did *not* want that to be part of my story. I already had enough heartache. I did not need to add divorce to my litany of experiences. But, as it did for many, the pandemic created a vacuum life for Lyssa and me, and the challenges we already faced became magnified by being together 24/7 without family support or outside guidance. Issues and warning signs that had been rumbling beneath the surface, really for our entire relationship, intensified in a way that could no longer be ignored or brushed aside. We sought help and found one of the best therapists I've ever seen. But rather than being a catalyst for change, it brought things to a boiling point. A few months in, the therapist informed me that the relationship had become dangerous and if things didn't change soon, we needed to part ways.

Things didn't change. Almost before I knew what was happening, it escalated to the point that I was deeply afraid for my safety and found myself secretly packing an emergency bag late one night, and putting steps in place in case I needed to get out quickly with the dogs. I was terrified and felt like I was suddenly in an alternative reality.

Just a few weeks later, I was in group therapy. I sat in horror and utter shock as I listened to the other members' stories and how closely they mirrored mine. *How the fuck did I end up here?* I kept asking myself. *Why does everything they say resonate so deeply?*

It's easy to feel like I failed, or for those against queer marriages to pin the blame on us, saying, "You shouldn't have gotten married in the first place." The reality is, any time we enter into a relationship of any kind, we take a risk. There's no way for any of us to ever know what the full outcome of that relationship will be. We cannot change or control other people, nor can we predict the future. We can only do our best to lean into love with the information we have in the moment and what we feel and believe to be true at that time in our lives. With almost 50 percent of marriages in the United States ending in divorce, a commitment to love is always going to be a gamble of the heart. But that doesn't mean we shouldn't love. Love takes courage. It takes bravery. It takes grit (especially as queer people) to say, "I'm in this relationship with you and I'm willing to take the risk of giving us a try." We have no idea what that could mean or hold.

We learn important things about ourselves when we are willing to put our hearts on the line and do hard things, even when we're afraid. As brutal as these last couple years have been, I've learned a great deal—about myself, about what I want and need in a partner, and about my own becoming and belonging to myself. I've learned so much that they will likely be books unto themselves.

It's important for you to know, though, that I still 100 percent believe in and champion queer marriages. My experience does not change that. I also believe that we don't necessarily have to subscribe to heteronormative life milestones in order to find success, happiness, or achievement. Just because society says we have to be straight, White, thin, and beautiful; have a career; and be married with 2.5 kids doesn't mean that those things actually equal success or happiness. Happiness, joy, and peace can only be found and fulfilled deep within ourselves. Sometimes finding those parts of ourselves takes time.

My marriage to Lyssa did not turn out the way I dreamed or thought it would. I've worked through (and am still working through) many things as I process the grief of losing my marriage. LGBTQ+ people have multilayered trauma. Complexly woven through multiple layers of internalized homophobia/transphobia, purity culture, conversion therapy, family rejection, religious trauma, and lack of parental support, the cards are stacked against us from the start when it comes to relationships. Yet love is the very thing we've been longing for (and likely losing in multiple areas) all of our lives. To risk entering a relationship at all is to bravely believe that love is worth fighting (and possibly failing) for.

I took the risk of believing in love based on what I felt, knew, and believed to be right at the time. That's all any of us can really do.

When my marriage ended in the fall of 2021, I made a choice to move back to Colorado Springs, at least for a season. It's not something I ever dreamed I would do, yet it felt right at the time and I had to trust that. But I was skeptical. I was concerned about the conservative nature of the town and didn't know if it was possible for Colorado Springs to have changed. I chose a quiet little corner known as a more progressive part of the city, and started my life over for the second time.

On one of the first days that I went on a walk with my dogs, I had on a T-shirt that said something "softly gay." It definitely wasn't my shirt that proclaims in big, bold letters, "The future is queer!" but something like "Love who you are" with a little rainbow heart. Still, I wondered to myself, *Am I safe to wear this here? Will this make me a target for hate?*

I carefully dipped my toes in the water to try and get a temperature of the town. What I discovered was interesting and unexpected: those who were queer and grew up here under the oppressive shadow of conservative evangelicalism had the same scars from religious trauma that I did, but those who moved here by choice were having an overall positive experience in this outdoorsy city at the base of the Rocky Mountains. I was pleasantly surprised and began slowly prying my mind open to positive experiences.

I can't say that living in Colorado Springs has been completely anxiety-free. With the knowledge that my parents still live in this town and that a handful of extended family have also moved here in recent years, I am keenly aware that I could run into them at any time, especially in the more northern parts of the city. It's been more than eleven years since I came out, more than nine since my dad said he couldn't handle the drama anymore and completely cut ties, and I still have no contact with my parents, brother, or any extended family.

My dream, of course, especially in the early years, was that my family would eventually "come around." While I do still wish that for them because I believe their lives would be richer, freer, and more authentic if they were able to see a God bigger than their box, I've also had to let go of that hope for change and move on with finding meaning in my own life apart from them. Early on, I hoped that when my dad survived two open-heart surgeries in a week's time, it would cause him to reevaluate priorities. When that didn't happen, I thought that the division we experienced in our country during the Trump presidency might cause them to reconsider. When COVID-19 hit, I swore if anything would cause them to think about what really matters, a worldwide pandemic would, especially during those first few months when the entire world was shut down. But when all these things came and went and nothing changed, I had to let go of hope. I had to come to terms with and accept the fact that their views and beliefs will likely never change.

Hope can be dangerous for LGBTQ+ people. For queer people who have lost so much, holding onto hope—whether it's for birth family to come around or even for chosen family to fill a gap—can set them up for repeatedly exposing themselves not just to disappointment, but also to being retraumatized when things don't work out the way they want (or hope) for them to. Finding a balance between what is potentially healing and what is potentially harmful is a tricky task.

Even when the Club Q shooting happened, a small part of me wondered if perhaps *that* would be their turning point. But the reality is, even if they were to embrace full inclusion and affirm LGBTQ+ relationships at this point in their lives, our relationship will never be what it could have and should have been. We will never have the closeness, the trust, the familial bond we could have shared had they done the hard work up front. More than a decade of life has passed. Big things have come and gone. I've moved on and found meaning in the chosen family that surrounds me, and my two pups continue to provide me with love and joy daily.

Half Pint is now fourteen and slowly transitioned into retirement during the pandemic, a necessary but hard transition for us both. She is now spoiled with daily walks, plenty of treats and belly rubs, and copious amounts of sunbeaming. Our bond remains very close, and she continues to save me in ways that are hard to put into words.

I've been pleasantly surprised at the number of affirming faith communities that are popping up in Colorado Springs. Following the shooting at Club Q, the affirming faith leaders in the city wrote a letter urging political, civic, and faith leaders to end harmful LGBTQ+ messages in the Pikes Peak region and beyond. It was signed by more than fifty clergy.[1]

Personally, my faith has continued on a journey of evolution, deconstruction, and discovery. I still value faith, relationship with Spirit, and meaningful community very much. While I still work with churches and at the intersection of faith and sexuality a great deal, I do not currently attend church myself. My own journey of religious trauma has slowly brought me to find spirituality outside the structure of organized religion. I've long said that you do not have to be in church to find or know God. God is everywhere, in all things, at all times. We need only to be open to and aware of it. What I find most meaningful and enriching in this season is conversations with other open-minded people about faith and life. I've seen it build rich and lasting community that is deeply life-giving. I also find beauty and have always deeply connected with the Divine in nature. It quiets my soul, grounds me, and allows me to hear the still, soft voice of God, if only I take the time to listen. These things are my church, my experience of connecting with and to the Spirit both within me and all around me. These are the ways of discovering God beyond the confines of buildings, services, and restrictions that feel safe and life-giving to me. This is where I find the ability to be free, and fully me.

Sitting on the sidelines as the Pride parade floats passed one by one, it felt like my story was coming full circle in a way. The hometown I moved away from after coming out was now celebrating my existence alongside me. At the parade, which had been reinstated after a two-year break during the pandemic, the energy was electric, families were celebrating with their young children, and I passed only two people being rude. I considered that a win. It was a beautiful day with beautiful weather and beautiful people, celebrating a beautiful thing called love. Previous attendees told me that this year's parade was the most robust they'd seen.

I don't expect Colorado Springs to be my forever home, but I do wonder if coming back here for a season is a critical component of my own healing. I also feel that part of why I am here is to raise awareness and be a voice for those growing up here who can't yet speak or advocate for themselves.

Coming out of FOTF, I never dreamed I'd return to the town that caused me such pain and anguish. I never thought that sharing my story would lead me back to my roots. But each of us is on a journey of becoming and belonging.

When we are becoming, we are leaning into the truth of who we were meant to be at our core. We let go of expectations that others have for us. We let go of expectations we have for ourselves. We stop looking at who the world tells us we are supposed to be and instead love and nurture who we really are, bringing our most authentic selves to life.

When we are belonging, we are feeding our most authentic self with the nutrients that allow us to continue to thrive. There's no hiding in belonging—no filtering or masking or striving to impress. Only transparency, followed by full acceptance. When we are seeking belonging it's because we are *longing* to just *be*—to have a space where our full self is welcome and at rest. In this space, we can bring all of who we are and be accepted, celebrated, and loved. In this space, we know that who we are is enough.

Sometimes belonging comes in the form of like-minded community—people who see and affirm all of us. Sometimes belonging comes from within ourselves. Maya Angelou said, "You only are free when you realize you belong no place—you belong every place—no place at all."[2] This kind of freedom comes only by belonging, and believing, in oneself. Then, and only then, can we belong everywhere and nowhere all at once. Then, and only then, can we truly be free to live and love unashamed.

Me, age three, with James Dobson.

Will Ryan (the voice of Eugene Meltsner) and me.

Praying with my stuffed animals, age two.

*My first day
of school.*

*Winning a county-
wide talent competition
at age three for my
recitation of "The
Moon Came Too."*

*Performing
my first solo
piano recital,
age seven.*

My piano recital cake, when I was seven.

Performing my competition piece at an awards recital.

Paul Herlinger (the voice of Mr. Whittaker) and me.

Sitting with Santa Claus (aka Dad).

Performing at a Christian school.

Dressing up as Pippi Longstocking for Halloween.

Recording the "Adventures in Odyssey Live!" episode for the tenth-anniversary celebration.

Signing autographs at the Adventures in Odyssey *tenth-anniversary event held at Focus on the Family.*

Doing an Adventures in Odyssey *event for a Make a Wish Foundation child with Townsend Coleman (the voice of Jason Whittaker).*

Meet The "Green Gables Girls"

Me in my "Diana" dress with my Diana Doll

Wearing a new dress for one of our Green Gable Girls events.

My lifelong GGG friend Rebekah and me.

An American Girl party with my GGG friends.

Signing my purity pledge.

My purity ring and pledge signed on my thirteenth birthday.

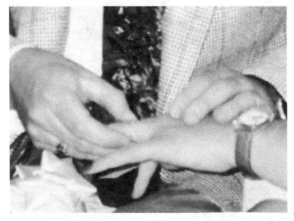

My dad placing my purity ring on my wedding finger.

At age fifteen, my thick eyebrows were nonexistent.

High school senior photo, age sixteen.

High school senior photo, age sixteen.

Leading worship at the prayer center.

Words I wrote on my arm to abstain from cutting.

*My basket
of rocks.*

Rocks used in therapy before I came out.

5-12-12

My worst fear has come true:

I've become an orphan.

Journal entry after I came out.

Bonding with Half Pint
during my darkest days.

Loading the
moving truck
for Denver.

*Performing with my
new church choir
at Denver Pride.*

*Half Pint becomes
a service dog.*

Bonding with Half Pint in Denver.

*Starting to use my story to be
a voice for others, 2017.*

*Half Pint on tour with me as I travel
and advocate for LGBTQ+ equality.*

(PHOTO CREDIT: ELLIE DOTE)

Unashamed *(the first LGBTQ+ Christian coming-out guide) releases in 2019.*

Diagnosed with Lyme disease on June 19, 2020. (Photo credit: Martha Wirth Photography)

Spending time with chosen family after moving back to Colorado Springs, 2022.

My fur babies and me.

Visiting the Club Q memorial just days
after the shooting, November 2022.

ACKNOWLEDGMENTS

To the entire WJK team: Thank you to each of you who invested your time and talents to help make this book what it is. I am grateful for the chance to give this project a new life and a new voice. You're a joy to partner with.

To my editor, Jessica Miller Kelley: Thank you for your insight, creativity, and patience in all the ways with all the things and for the stellar title. I appreciate your gentleness and the way we work and flow together.

To my Patreon Community who partner with me in this work toward a more just and loving society: Thank you for your continual support. I couldn't do this important work without you. You make what I do possible.

To my beta readers: Thank you for your insight, wisdom, experience, and feedback that helped shape the final drafts of this book.

To KreativEdge Photography: Thank you for gifting your time and talent to capture the headshot for this book's cover. You brought out the best in me when I wasn't sure there was any left.

To my Fab Five:

Stace—You've processed many a fucking hard thing with me and held space in the darkest of times. Vault buddies for life.

Jen—We've had so many conversations about this project and I'm so grateful for your practicality, wit, honesty, and deep wisdom. Thank you for walking along the ocean's shore with me and holding space for absolutely everything. It's the greatest gift I've ever been given.

Tiff—You've been a rock and constant presence of both emotional and practical support through the major life transitions of the last couple years. You seem to always know exactly what I need. Thank you . . . for each and every thing. You're the best heart sibling a person could ask for.

Rebekah—There's something invaluable about having a friend that's known you from the age of, what . . . eight? It's a gift that I treasure and do not take for granted. I'm deeply grateful for the unique understanding we have for each other's stories because of the experiences we shared in our youth. Thank you for continually sticking around for the ride.

April—Thank you for reminding me that this story still has a voice. Thank you for holding it with me and creating a safe space for *all* things. Your love, desire, and willingness to do all things *together* carries me.

To those doing the hard work of social justice alongside of me: I am grateful to have you as colleagues and to work alongside you for the love and acceptance of all LGBTQ+ people.

To the Unashamed Love Collective: You've become some of my closest friends. I'm so grateful for the sacred community we share in together.

Finally, to every queer person who writes, emails, or messages me and says that my work has made a difference: You're the reason I get out of bed and continue working for equality each day. Thank you for trusting me with the gift of hearing your stories in return. You are fully and deeply loved.

RECOMMENDED RESOURCES

Organizations
The Christian Closet
   www.thechristiancloset.com
Church Clarity
   www.churchclarity.org
Cultivating Community Retreats
   www.AmberCantornaWylde.com/retreats
Free Mom Hugs
   FreeMomHugs.org
Human Rights Campaign
   www.hrc.org
Mama Bears
   www.realmamabears.org
The Matthew Shepard Foundation
   www.matthewshepard.org
988 Suicide & Crisis Lifeline
   https://988lifeline.org/
1946: The Mistranslation That Shifted Culture
   www.1946themovie.com
PFLAG (Parents, Family and Friends of Lesbians and Gays)
   www.pflag.org
Q Christian Fellowship
   www.qchristian.org
Transmission Ministry Collective
   https://transmissionministry.com

Trans-Parenting
  https://www.trans-parenting.com
The Trevor Project
  www.thetrevorproject.com
Tyler Clementi Foundation
  https://tylerclementi.org
Unashamed Love Collective
  www.unashamedlovecollective.com

Recommended Reading

Baldock, Kathy. *Forging a Sacred Weapon.* Reno, NV: Canyon-walker Press, forthcoming.

———. *Walking the Bridgeless Canyon.* Reno, NV: Canyon-walker Press, 2015.

Beeching, Vicky. *Undivided.* New York: HarperOne, 2018.

Cantorna, Amber. *Unashamed.* Louisville, KY: Westminster John Knox Press, 2019.

Chomiak, Stacey. *Still Stace.* Minneapolis: Beaming Books, 2021.

Gushee, David. *Changing Our Mind.* Canton, MI: Read the Spirit Books, 2017.

Hartke, Austen. *Transforming: Updated and Expanded Edition with Study Guide.* Louisville, KY: Westminster John Knox Press, 2023.

Martin, Colby. *UnClobber Expanded Edition with Study Guide.* Louisville, KY: Westminster John Knox Press, 2022.

Riley, Reba. *Post-Traumatic Church Syndrome.* New York: Howard Books, 2016.

For a more comprehensive resource list, please visit my website at www.AmberCantornaWylde.com.

NOTES

CHAPTER 1: MY ADVENTURE IN ODYSSEY

1. "Foundational Values," Focus on the Family, May 31, 2019, https://www.focusonthefamily.com/about/foundational -values/.

2. Paul R. Spittzeri, "The Slippery Slope of Social Engineering: The Case of Paul B. Popenoe, 1915–1930," Homestead Museum, February 27, 2020, https://homesteadmuseum .blog/2020/02/27/the-slippery-slope-of-social-engineering-the -case-of-paul-b-popenoe-1915-1930/.

3. Edwin Black, "Eugenics and the Nazis—The California Connection," *SFGATE*, November 9, 2003, https:// www.sfgate.com/opinion/article/Eugenics-and-the-Nazis-the -California-2549771.php.

4. Rick Pidcock, "There's a Straight Line from Eugenics to 'Biblical Family Values' to White Supremacy and the Anti-abortion Movement," Baptist News Global, July 5, 2022, https:// baptistnews.com/article/theres-a-straight-line-from-eugenics -to-biblical-family-values-to-white-supremacy-and-the-anti -abortion-movement/.

5. Bobby Burke and Horace Gerlach, "Daddy's Little Girl," recorded by the Mills Brothers in 1950.

6. *The Ties That Bind* (Tyndale Entertainment, 2014).

CHAPTER 3: THE HARMS OF PURITY CULTURE

1. Descriptive copy of Joshua Harris, *I Kissed Dating Goodbye* (Sisters, OR: Multnomah, 1999), audio CD, https://www.amazon.com/Kissed-Dating-Goodbye-Attitude-Relationships/dp/1576735907/.
2. Descriptive copy of Joshua Harris, *I Kissed Dating Goodbye* (Sisters, OR: Multnomah, 2003), https://www.amazon.com/Kissed-Dating-Goodbye-Joshua-Harris/dp/1590521358.
3. "Unashamed Love and Community: Conversations with Amber Cantorna," YouTube, streamed live on February 14, 2022, https://www.youtube.com/watch?v=zSxPamKB_mM.

CHAPTER 5: WHEN MENTAL HEALTH IS TABOO

1. "Mental Health Disparities: LGBTQ," American Psychiatric Association, 2017, https://www.psychiatry.org/File%20Library/Psychiatrists/Cultural-Competency/Mental-Health-Disparities/Mental-Health-Facts-for-LGBTQ.pdf.
2. Bessel A. van der Kolk, *The Body Keeps the Score: Brain, Mind, and Body in the Healing of Trauma*, https://www.besselvanderkolk.com/resources/the-body-keeps-the-score.

CHAPTER 6: DEFYING GENDER NORMS AND SOCIAL EXPECTATIONS

1. For detail on Focus on the Family's moral standards for employees, see https://media.focusonthefamily.com/fotf/pdf/about-us/human-resources/moral-policy.pdf.
2. "Focus Employees Say Hallelujah to New Dress Code," *Denver Post*, June 17, 2009, https://www.denverpost.com/2009/06/17/focus-employees-say-hallelujah-to-new-dress-code/.

CHAPTER 8: THE SACRED WEAPON

1. *1946: The Mistranslation That Shifted Culture,* directed by Sharon "Rocky" Roggio, 2022, https://www.1946themovie.com/.

2. Kathy Baldock, "As a 21-Year-Old Seminarian, David Fearon Challenged the RSV Translators on the Word 'Homosexual,'" Baptist News Global, January 10, 2023, https://baptistnews.com/article/as-a-21-year-old-seminarian-david-fearon-challenged-the-rsv-translators-on-the-word-homosexual/.

3. "Facts about LGBTQ Youth Suicide," The Trevor Project, December 15, 2021, https://www.thetrevorproject.org/resources/article/facts-about-lgbtq-youth-suicide/.

CHAPTER 9: UNDOING THE DAMAGE OF CONVERSION THERAPY

1. Jonathan Merritt, "The Downfall of the Ex-Gay Movement," *Atlantic,* October 6, 2015, https://www.theatlantic.com/politics/archive/2015/10/the-man-who-dismantled-the-ex-gay-ministry/408970/.

2. "Equality Maps: Conversion 'Therapy' Laws," Movement Advancement Project, last modified March 31, 2023, https://www.lgbtmap.org/equality-maps/conversion_therapy.

3. *Pray Away,* directed by Kristine Stolakis (Multitude Films, 2021).

4. "Facts about LGBTQ Youth Suicide," The Trevor Project, December 15, 2021, https://www.thetrevorproject.org/resources/article/facts-about-lgbtq-youth-suicide/; "LGB People Who Have Undergone Conversion Therapy Almost Twice as Likely to Attempt Suicide," Williams Institute at UCLA School of Law, June 15, 2020, https://williamsinstitute.law.ucla.edu/press/lgb-suicide-ct-press-release/.

5. Brené Brown, "Shame vs. Guilt," *From Brené*, January 15, 2013, https://brenebrown.com/articles/2013/01/15/shame -v-guilt/.

CHAPTER 10: BREAKING FREE FROM
CHRISTIAN NATIONALISM

1. Brittanica, s.v. "Moral Majority," last updated February 12, 2018, https://www.britannica.com/topic/Moral-Majority.

2. Sara Savat, "Cultural Backlash: Is LGBTQ Progress an Attack on Christianity?," *The Source,* Washington University in St. Louis, August 26, 2021, https://source.wustl.edu/2021/08 /cultural-backlash-is-lgbtq-progress-an-attack-on-christianity/.

3. "Franklin Graham and Dr. Dobson Q&A," *Family Talk* podcast, January 19, 2016, https://www.drjamesdobson.org /broadcasts/franklin-graham-and-dr-dobson-q-a.

4. Judith Kohler, "500 Gay Rights Supporters Protest outside Focus," *Casper (WY) Star-Tribune,* May 2, 2005, http://trib.com/news/state-and-regional/gay-rights-supporters -protest-outside-focus/article_69f9cdbe-0100-5e5d-928e -f7c9611b55df.html.

5. "The Trevor Project Research Brief: Accepting Adults Reduce Suicide Attempts among LGBTQ Youth," The Trevor Project,June2019,https://www.thetrevorproject.org/wp-content /uploads/2019/06/Trevor-Project-Accepting-Adult-Research -Brief_June-2019.pdf.

CHAPTER 13: BECOMING AN ORPHAN

1. James Dobson, "Speaking the Truth in Love," Dobson Digital Library, https://dobsonlibrary.com/resource/article /ac7f7f93-2df0-4b8d-8511-0b85e46dc9f7.

CHAPTER 14: THE DEADLY EFFECTS
OF TOXIC THEOLOGY

1. An example can be seen at https://www.focusonthefamily
.com/family-qa/responding-to-teen-child-who-says-hes-gay/
2. Jonah DeChants, Amy E. Green, Myeshia N. Price, and
Carrie Davis, "Homelessness and Housing Instability among
LGBTQ Youth," The Trevor Project, 2021, https://www.the
trevorproject.org/wp-content/uploads/2022/02/Trevor-Project
-Homelessness-Report.pdf.
3. "Youth at Greater Risk of Experiencing Homelessness,"
Chapin Hall at the University of Chicago, https://www.chapin
hall.org/wp-content/uploads/National-Estimates_Youth-at
-Greater-Risk-of-Experiencing-Homelessness.png.

CHAPTER 16: CHOOSING LOVE

1. John 10:10.

CHAPTER 17: BEGINNING TO LIVE
WITH CHRONIC ILLNESS

1. Lindsey Dawson, Brittni Frederiksen, Michelle Long,
Usha Ranji, and Jennifer Kates, "LGBT+ People's Health and
Experiences Accessing Care," Women's Health Policy, Kai-
ser Family Foundation, July 22, 2021, https://www.kff.org
/report-section/lgbt-peoples-health-and-experiences-accessing
-care-report/.
2. "Resources," The Quiet Epidemic, https://www.the
quietepidemic.com/resources-and-evidence.
3. Daniel Lynch, "Why Is Lyme Disease Not Covered by
Insurance," Bay Area Lyme Foundation, September 28, 2017,

https://www.bayarealyme.org/blog/lyme-disease-not-covered
-insurance/#:~:text=%E2%80%9CAs%20insurance%20
companies%20rely%20on,systematically%20deny%20
claims%20associated%20with.

CHAPTER 18: HOMETOWN PRIDE

1. Lindsey Grewe, "Pikes Peak Region Clergy Write Letter Affirming Support for LGBTQ+ Community in Wake of Club Q Shooting," KKTV, November 27, 2022, https://www.kktv.com/2022/11/27/pikes-peak-region-clergy-write-letter-affirming-support-lgbtq-community-wake-club-q-shooting/.

2. Maya Angelou, interview by Bill Moyers, *Bill Moyers Journal*, PBS, November 21, 1973, https://billmoyers.com/content/conversation-maya-angelou/.

(Photo credit: KreativEdge Photography)

To support the continuation of Amber Cantorna-Wylde's work, consider joining Patreon—the community of people who partner with Amber to work toward a more just and loving world for LGBTQ+ people. Learn more at Patreon.com/AmberCantornaWylde. To see Amber's current projects, visit her website at AmberCantornaWylde.com and follow her on social media @AmberCantornaWylde.

9 780664 267957